It's just f

C000079668

round th

A non-runner's journey

to her first marathon

By Helen Stothard

First published 2013

www.hlspublishing.com

ISBN: 978-1484968444

Copyright © Helen Stothard

All rights reserved. No part of this publication may be reproduced, stored or transmitted in any form, or by any means, electronic, mechanical or photocopying, recording or otherwise, without express written permission of the author.

Limit of Liability/Disclaimer of Warranty: This book is designed to provide information about the subject matter. It is sold with the understanding that the publisher and authors are not engaged in rendering legal, coaching or other professional services. While the publisher and author have used their best efforts in preparing this book, they make no representations or warranties with respect to the accuracy or completeness of the contents of this book and specifically disclaim any implied warranties of merchantability or fitness for a particular purpose. No warranty may be created or extended by sales representatives or written sales materials. This book is not intended or should be a substitute for therapy or professional advice. The views and opinions expressed in this page are strictly those of the author. The advice and strategies contained herein may not be suitable for your situation. The publisher is not engaged in rendering professional services, and you should consult a competent professional where appropriate. Neither the publisher nor author shall be liable for any loss of profit or any other commercial damages, including but not limited to special, incidental, consequential, or other damages. This document is provided for educational purposes only. The reader assumes all risk and responsibility for the usage of any information or ideas contained in this guide. If you do not wish to be bound by the above, you may return the book to the publisher for a full refund.

London Marathon Race photos: marathonfoto.com
Brass Monkey photo: The Race Photographer

Dedications

This book has to be dedicated to Dennis, aka Simon Pegg, from the movie Run Fat Boy Run. Dennis was tired of being a nearly man; he wasn't fat, he was just unfit; and he inspired me to want to run a marathon one day.

Huge thanks, or should it be blame, to my brother Jamie Wells, who was daft enough to mutter the immortal words "We should enter Castle Howard 10k" which is what really started this crazy journey.

Thank you, to my husband Ian and my gorgeous daughter Kirsty for putting up with my running madness; it's no fun for them ferrying me to races then standing around in the cold waiting for me to finish. Kirsty has even kept me company on a few of my training runs and joined in a couple of races.

To Charley Watkins, Sam Lyth, Michelle Poole, Karen Garbutt, Gail Harvey, Louise Sherlock, Darren Reevell, Helen Reevell, Kate Akrill Misso, Kelly Jackson, the rest of the Fetch Everyone community, Cathy Grisdale, Rob Oliver, Shaun Imeson, Dee Bouderba, Moz Marathon Man Render, Simon Partridge, Bill Shively, Heather Bulmer and the rest of the gang at York Postal Harriers and all the other runners I've failed to mention who have supported me on my journey, either by joining me on a run or just being there with advice and support.

And to my 'Naughty Table' who always encouraged me to believe and once even made me get my trainers out for a run after a long break; they were there for me on the days it didn't go quite so well. Thank you Sarah, Carole, Rachel and Roz.

Huge thanks go to Anne Fieldhouse, the lady who made me cry by showing me the kindness of strangers.

To my Mother, Sue Wells, because hearing you tell me how proud of me you were was something beyond special.

Thank you.

Lastly, in memory of little Alfie Oliver, 50p from the sale of each book will be donated to Martin House Children's Hospice – sleep well Alfie xx

Praise for 'It's just four times round the village'

Absolutely brilliant read....if it doesn't inspire you to get out and run, nothing will. An amazing story by an inspirational lady who can prove that if she can do it, anyone can!!

I'm proud and honoured to be able to call you my friend - Well done. I have tears in my eyes reading the last chapter....just like on the day :)
Gail Harvey

Helen wouldn't be my friend, nor would have I been included in her journey, had it not been for running! To read of the epic challenge emotionally, mentally and physically in order to get to completing a marathon offers inspiration and encouragement to anyone who thinks "*I would like to try that, but I don't think I can*". I've been there, done that, got the t-shirt and the medals BUT not a London one yet! I look forward to doing a marathon with you in the future!

I read this cover to cover in a space of 24 hours-inspirational, encouraging and practical. If you don't think you can then read this. And remember Helen, 1 down 99 to go!"
Kelly Jackson BSc Hons

Contents

Disclaimer

One thing that will become apparent when you read this book is that I am not a specialist. Truth be told I am not sure I even have a clue what I am doing.

Therefore, my advice to you, before you undertake any form of exercise, is speak to a specialist, be that your Doctor or physiotherapist. Find out the right way to do it.

Most of this book is me telling you what I did wrong. Yes, I finally achieved my dream but if I'd taken the time to listen to the people who knew what they were talking about instead of trying to make it up as I went along and being such a stubborn old bugger, who knows how much sooner that could have happened.

In the almost five years I've been running I've been on the injured bench more than I've been fit and well.

So... take no notice of anything I say and seek professional advice.

Nuff said.

Introduction

I suppose this story really starts for me when I was 39. I'd just watched the movie 'Run Fat Boy Run' and loved it. Who doesn't love an underdog!

I'd never been sporty really; at school I took part in hockey, netball, high jump and the 400m but only because I was told I had to, and never as part of a team, just during PE classes and sports day.

After leaving school I did the odd aerobics class or badminton, but even that faded away when I bought my first house at the age of 22. From then on it all went downhill as fast as my waist band expanded!

I'd never grown up with an athletic influence in my close family, never known anyone who ran, never mind anyone who'd run a marathon.

When I was 21 I was diagnosed with ME, or Post Viral Fatigue Syndrome. I'd always been a sickly child, prone to viruses, German Measles and even Glandular Fever. Luckily I was back at work in just over six months and I seem to be managing it fairly well now, as long as I am sensible and don't overdo it.

Over the years I'd taken part in some small fun runs or the Race for Life, but always as a run walker; in other words I'd run too fast then have to walk for ages to get my breath back, and I'd never achieved anything further than 5k (or 3.1 miles if you're like my mother and want that translating into English!)

I'd started to watch others, including my sister-in-law, Charley, go from fun runs to 10ks to marathons. I wanted to do it but just didn't think I had it in me. Let's just say Charley is slim, blonde, fit and runs marathons - there's no comparison between us at all, so there was no reason to suppose I would ever follow in her footsteps and take part in a marathon.

From being a small child I'd always watched London Marathon from the comfort of my sofa and always thought I'd love to take part one day, never believing that one day I'd get to make that dream come true.

So there we are, in the early spring of 2008, my little brother watches 'Run Fat Boy Run' then comes out with the magic words 'I think we should do Castle Howard 10k'.

Whilst Jamie wasn't a runner, and was and still is very fond of his Magners, he did play a lot of football. By this point in my life I'd become a Mum, totally foregone any form of exercise, other than walking to the fridge for chocolate, and was probably (okay definitely) overweight and very unfit.

This isn't a book that spans just a year like many first-time marathon stories I have read, truth is, it took me a long time to get to that marathon start line, nearly five years in fact; this is a book written for people like me, who never intended to start running and simply didn't have a clue what it would entail, or how on earth to go about it.

Now a 10k isn't something you enter without practice and this is where our story begins...

Starting the Journey

'Eek' is probably a much more polite phrase than the one I really used when this was first suggested to me. I could barely manage 5k round a flat racecourse as it was, and someone somewhere just happened to mention that Castle Howard has a hill!

I was sensible enough to download the Cancer Research 10k training plan when I signed up for the 10k. I'd like to say I was sensible enough to follow it to the letter, but hey, we're talking about me here!

The plan starts you off walking, gradually introducing the running over time, until at the end you can run the whole 10k distance. Okay, I might have missed out some of the walking, and I definitely got a bit over-confident, and as a result I buggered my ankle.

In June of 2008 we went on holiday to Salou. There I was up at early o'clock every morning going for my run while the rest of them were in bed. Okay, run/walk, but those runs were some of the best running memories I have. Running down by the beach, most of Salou still in their beds, the street cleaners out washing the streets, the nightclubs just getting out, the sky was blue, the sand was clean and it was heaven.

Compare that to a few weeks later when I was back in the village running through the woods and dodging slugs!

Where you run can really make a difference.

LESSON: Never think you know better than the training plan!

Running Kit

Now I'm sure that you've all read somewhere that all you need to run is a pair of trainers.

Let me stop you there.

Dennis may have felt it appropriate to wear a pair of swimming trunks instead of shorts in his first run to the end of the street in 'Run Fat Boy Run' but even he realised that running in the wrong kit causes problems.

The most important piece of running kit is your trainers. You really should get 'Gait Analysis' from your local running shop and have trainers fitted. This involves running on a treadmill in different shoes to find the pair that best suit your running style.

You may hear about pronation, neutral, support and the rest. What it boils down to is that you need to wear the right style of trainer to match your style of running. Although I started out in a neutral trainer (no support) I am now on support trainers due to all the injuries I've suffered that have changed my running style over the years.

The difference the right trainers make is unbelievable. Wear the wrong ones and you'll suffer injury and shin splints. Both hurt. (Another do as I say not do as I do example from my early days in running.)

I don't buy my trainers from the internet, and believe me I am the Internet Shopping Queen! I go to my specialist shop and get professional advice. It costs me more, but it's worth every penny. I also get the advantage of a 30 day return policy as well, so if I take my new trainers out on a run and they're not right for me I can change them.

If you're a female runner then the next most important piece of running kit is your running bra. If you're on the well-endowed side like me, let's just say double letters that are on the wrong side of E with a smallish back size, this is even more essential. You cannot run comfortably if everything is bouncing around down there. I've seen some women running with so much bounce I'm surprised they don't knock themselves out! It's not just the damage you'll do to your bust either, it will affect your neck and back as well.

You can buy proper sports bras that are sized like your regular bra and support you properly. Or you can do what I did when I started out on a budget and just buy a sports bra style crop top in a size smaller which holds everything so flat in place it can't move. The downside to this is the battle you have to get the thing on and off!

You don't have to have special running tights or running tops, but if you can afford them then they are certainly more comfortable to wear.

Now we're having a marathon in York for the first time, half the village is out running in kit they've bought from the local discount sports outlet. There's nothing wrong with it, it does the job, and if I'm paying I often go there as well, but if someone else is paying then I go to one of the dedicated sports retailers and buy one of the running brands. They all do the same job, they don't make you a faster runner, but I have to say the more expensive stuff does make me feel like a better runner and fits more comfortably.

Don't buy kit if you don't need it; the sports shops are full of stuff to tempt you, and I have a case full of such purchases that never see the light of day. Buy things as you need them, read reviews and ask for advice on a running forum such as Fetch Everyone.

LESSON: The right trainers can make a huge difference

Race for Life July 2008

This was the first time my daughter had agreed to run with me, and the first race she'd done.

At five years old she was so excited about taking part, shopping for trainers and her Race for Life T-shirt (my bank balance wasn't quite as eager!)

Sadly, the weather wasn't on our side at all. Just before the warm up the heavens opened, and stayed that way. It wasn't helped by the usual Race for Life late start.

We were soaked to the skin before we set off, yet my daughter was an absolute star the whole way round.

I don't think we truly realised just how wet and cold it was until we'd finished. I've taken clothes out of the washing machine after the wash cycle that have been dryer than the clothes we were wearing when we crossed that finish line!

Sadly, it was several years before my daughter would consider running with me again.

LESSON: Always take dry spare clothes with you to a race no matter how short it is.

RESULT: Distance - 5K. Time: 55 mins approx

York Millennium Bridge 5k August 2008

This was my first 'proper' race. It's organised by one of the local running clubs and is very different to the more social Race for Life 5ks.

The race was in two parts due to the route, and meant the faster runners wouldn't be held up by people like me! The fast runners set off first and then about 15 minutes later the rest of us set off.

The route starts on one side of the river in the city of York, goes twice round a park, over the Millennium Bridge and then back down the other side of the river to the finish.

There had been talk that the race might be cancelled due to the very wet weather but it went ahead; it's also where I met one of my Fetch Everyone running friends for the first time - Kate aka Too Lilac.

Despite this being a race organised by a running club there was quite a good camaraderie at the start line (least ways there was at the back where I was).

I did my usual run/walk and was really pleased with my finish time, although my husband did point out that both the old man and the old lady taking part had beaten me. I seem to recall that I may have been last but one, but I wasn't last!

LESSON: Don't worry about what the other runners are doing, just try and do your best

RESULT: Distance - 5K. Time: 36:25

Fetch Yorkshire Miles

If you've never heard of Fetch Everyone do go check it out: http://www.fetcheveryone.com

It's an online forum and website for runners.

I came across it in summer 2008 when looking for some support and advice in preparation for the Castle Howard 10k.

The people on there were so supportive and welcoming, and it was a much more light-hearted and less serious forum than Runners World which had left me feeling rather daunted.

You can record your training, your race portfolio and even blog on there.

The guys on Fetch Everyone cover everything from the total novice like me to people who do marathons, ultra marathons, triathlons and even do 10 marathons in 10 days. There is no snobbery, no making you feel inadequate, just a sense of welcome and community.

If you're cautious about joining a 'proper' running club they have their own online running club (FERC) which is optional, and for an annual fee you can become a member and get the affiliated status from UK Athletics that gets you discount on your race entry as well as discounts from some running suppliers.

I joined FERC for a short period while I was making my mind up over whether to join a local club or not.

Every so often the guys on Fetch get together and organise regional 'miles'.

We all turn up at the track and have a bash at seeing how fast we can run a mile. Then we eat cake. Then we go to the pub for beer. I can see the smile on your face already!

They're real family occasions, we take the kids along, we have a good natter, we take lots of photos, eat and drink, and somewhere in all of that we run.

My first mile was in August 2008 and I took part in several more over the next few months.

LESSON: Join in social events like this, the support is invaluable

RESULTS: Distance 1 mile

August 2008 Time: 11:58

November 2008 Time: 9:58

March 2009 Time: 9:17 (yes I did throw up!)

Finding time to run

A lot of people tell me they can't run as they can't find the time in their schedule. I disagree; with most of them, if they wanted to they could. It's all about being creative.

When you first start out you're probably only looking at half an hour, surely you can get up half an hour earlier to go for a run, or spend half an hour less in front of the TV? If you haven't got childcare, ask a neighbour, relative or a friend to spare you half an hour.

I started getting up at 6am so I could fit in my run before my husband went to work, ensuring I'd be back in time to look after my daughter.

I was working full time, had a daughter to get to school and I still found that half hour to run.

So be totally honest with yourself. If you wanted to find half an hour to do something fun you'd do it, so make the effort to find time for your run. Before you know it you'll be enjoying it, and feeling good about the rest of your day because you know you've already managed to get your run in while everyone else was in bed!

I am one of those people who prefer to run early morning; I've tried afternoons and evenings and to be honest it doesn't work for me. That said, if that's the only time I can find my half hour, then that's when I run.

LESSON: If you want something enough you'll always find a way.

Sutton Seven September 2008

I entered this race, I suppose, thinking that at seven miles it was further than the upcoming Castle Howard 10k and that if I could do this I wouldn't show myself up in front of the rest of the family I'd be running with.

By the time the race came round I had still only managed a 2 min walk/2 minute run routine, and the furthest distance I had covered to date was 3.65 miles.

Reading back over old blog posts I do wonder whether I had any sanity left when I decided to take part!

I'd been under the weather for the past few weeks and wasn't sure that having entered the race I should actually go through with it. However, I decided I'd rather take part and drop out than not try at all so off we went.

I started out well and tried to keep pace with a lady in a pink top who wasn't quite as fast as the other runners. I didn't quite make the first mile at her pace but did run most of it and that was the furthest I had run yet.

Just past the first mile I started to feel tired and achy but someone behind me commented 'hey, you're not taking my last place!' It was an older gentleman who was road walking. He was keeping a steady pace, and using my run/walk technique I managed to keep just ahead of him. Before I knew it we'd covered three miles.

At this point (my least favourite point in any race it has to be said) the 'proper' runners were already on their way back, and as I hit the three mile mark they were at the six mile mark.

Suddenly I hit the detour, one of the roads was closed so we were diverted back onto the airfield. I can't say it was the most picturesque of routes, and the countryside smelled fairly ripe! The airfield track was awful but there was worse to come. Just past the four mile mark the track turned into huge chunks of white gravel, a lethal combination, even walking felt dangerous and uncomfortable.

Needless to say my ankle went, and this in turn upset the hip. Still I'd hit the four mile mark so was rather pleased to have actually achieved a new distance for me. By five miles we were finally back on the road and thank God for a water station - one mouthful and I poured the rest of it over my head!

The hobble became worse, but rightly or wrongly (probably wrongly but I'll never change), I was determined to finish and my walk/hobble can't have been too slow as I managed to finish just ahead of the road walker behind me. Only just, mind.

I was so glad to see that finish line, and can't say I ran over it as much as ran/dragged myself over it.

The marshals were all very friendly and encouraging but this wasn't a race for a novice - being at the rear of the pack for all of the race is very demoralising. If I hadn't had the road walker behind me to encourage me I am pretty sure I would have quit.

The runners in front of me were so far ahead they were like dots on the horizon.

Regardless, I was so chuffed with myself to have finished and achieved a better time than I had expected, especially as the last two miles hurt.

It did make me feel better about the upcoming 10k which was now only a couple of weeks away, and at least I now knew I could cover the distance.

LESSON: Be wary of entering races early on that are full of club runners, they take their racing seriously and if you can't keep up with them it won't be a pleasant experience for you.

RESULT: Distance - 7 Miles Time - 1:27:25

Joining the Gym

I joined the gym in early October 2008 and remember being so excited the first time I ran for 10 minutes on the treadmill without stopping. It's the longest I'd ever managed.

I joined the gym as it was just too dark to run at 6am on a morning, and as part of my route has no path I didn't feel safe anymore.

I was surprised how many people were at the gym as soon as it opens at 6:30 on a morning. As I had to get home before my husband went to work it only left me half an hour on the treadmill.

I did a 5 minute walking warm up on an incline of 2, ran for ten minutes, walked for 5 minutes, ran for 5 minutes and then did a cool down. It was a much slower speed than I thought but at least I was running.

I prefer running outside but that morning was cold, foggy and dark so the gym was a welcome change.

LESSON: If you join a gym make sure you use it. I once paid two years' membership fees and never set foot through the door.

Lack of Support - October 2008

I had been looking at entering the Edinburgh Marathon which would fall on my 40th birthday weekend the following year. They had a team relay so I could join in and just complete part of it.

This is when the negative comments from those close to you start: 'You are doing too much', 'You are not ready for, not capable etc'. 'But I could do any of the four distances' said I, 'taking on more than you can do' said they'.

I had spent months telling myself I could do this, forcing myself to get out of bed and either run or go to the gym, pushing myself to get through a 5k, 7 miler, 10k and booking three half marathons for the following year.

I suppose it didn't help when I said I was reading a book that would get me marathon ready in eighteen weeks. I hadn't said I was doing the whole marathon though!.

Between this negativity and the 'I don't know how you do it', 'I couldn't do it' etc brigade from other friends and family, and let's not forget the classic 'you must be bloody mad!' how on earth I ever stayed motivated I shall never know!

I entered races to give me a goal to train for but I have to say it is bloody hard doing it solo.

I just had to keep telling myself how pleased I was at what I had done, and how I knew what I could do if I could stay positive and keep focused.

Don't you just love friends and family for taking the wind out of your sails? But don't listen to them, don't let anyone bring you down.

It's amazing how much difference time makes, and those same people did believe in me when I was training for London, and those same people were proud of me.

If I'd let the negative comments get to me back then, I'd never have achieved my dream, and it's a great feeling to prove all those early doubters wrong.

LESSON: Only listen to people who have something positive to say: you're going to be feeling negative enough without letting others bring you down.

Stretch it out

One thing I have learned over the past few years is the importance of stretching. For most of the time I never stretched before running, and believed that as I'd never done it I shouldn't start doing that later on, but in all that time I've always stretched when I got back from my run.

Okay, I lie, there's the odd time, but those are the times when I found I couldn't walk the next day, so if you don't want to look like a cowboy who's spent a long day riding on his horse and waddling around when you walk - stretch!

It's also a great way of preventing injury... okay, another bit of advice I ignored along the way as well!

If you're not sure what stretches to do I found the Cancer Research 10k training plan had some excellent stretches that I stuck with, as well as asking my sports massage guy for stretches that were more specific to my injury.

LESSON: Not stretching can cause injury.

Castle Howard 10k 2008

I'm not quite sure what happened, but come race day I wasn't ready for it. Now there's a surprise. My sister-in-law Charley and her husband Neil were also signed up to run with us.

I felt pretty sick most of the morning, which wasn't helped by the start being delayed by 20 minutes. Whilst I was used to late starts from the Race for Life 5ks, my sister-in-law tells me it isn't the same in the rest of the country. When the whole of the entry fee goes to admin (did you realise the charity doesn't get your entry fee?) I would have expected they would start on time.

I'm there all bouncy and positive with 'We'll finish this in 1 hour 15 minutes guys' to their muted mutterings about them not having done any training.

I'd only managed the first 1k when I decided I'd had enough! They wouldn't let me do my training plan of run 5 minutes/walk 5 minutes - I think I only managed 15 minutes of non-stop running (a first for me by the way) before I had to stop for a walk and catch my breath. Walking was awful, I had the most horrendous shin splint when I tried walking which wasn't apparent when I was running. However, I couldn't breathe and run all the way - Catch 22. We compromised by walking the hills and running the flats with me swearing and cursing my sister-in-law all the way.

By this point Jamie and Neil had tired of waiting for us (hold on, they never actually waited at all!) and shot off into the distance.

We came to a sharp bend and the Marshal advised not looking up - too late - I'd already seen the first hill from hell. The route had several hills and most of them were to be found in the second half.

The water station at 5k was very welcome, not for the drink, but so that I could dowse myself in cold water and cool off! It seemed to help in the second half despite the hills. I think it was more that I began to get control of my breathing than the effect of the water.

Just before the 9k mark we caught sight of the house again, what a beautiful view, I tried to suck my stomach in as I spotted a course photographer, but who was I kidding, it was taking all my energy just to run.

It wasn't an easy race for me, but it was my first 10k so will always be special, also because of the people who ran it with me.

I was so chuffed to finish and get my medal.

LESSON: If you can run your races with a friend do so, it makes it much easier than trying to do it all on your own, but go at your pace, don't let them drag you along.

RESULT: Distance - 10k Time: 1:18:52

I don't want to be fat and forty!

Having enjoyed Castle Howard in some sad and masochistic kind of way I decided that I wanted to carry on with this running lark.

The following May I would be turning 40, and the last thing I wanted was to be fat and 40!

I had this lovely image of a fit, fast running, slender looking me at my birthday party.

Shame real life gets in the way isn't it!

I entered three half marathons and other races for the following year, then life, injury and illness got in the way and I had to cancel them all.

LESSON: Set smaller, achievable, and shorter term goals to start with.

The hardest bit of running is getting off the sofa

I think that like many things in life, it's the thought of doing something that holds us back. We are a breed of procrastinators, we can always find a reason NOT to do something, it's much easier after all than finding a positive. Running falls into this category.

I have found that the hardest part of running is getting off the sofa.

There always seems to be an excuse why you can't just get up and go out for that run right now. There will be the odd occasion where that really is true, but are you just making excuses the rest of the time?

We tolerate things, it's habit. We imagine what will happen if we try and change a situation, and allow what we have imagined to dictate whether or not we change. Mention running to some people and they come up with dodgy knees, lack of exercise over many years, or the good old 'I can't run'. When was the last time you tried?

My running plan started me off walking. Now how many people can say that they can't walk?

The trick to any form of exercise is to do it at a pace and time that suits you.

I realised after three years that killing myself to get up at 6am and run before the school run wasn't something I needed to do any more. I was now self-employed so I could be flexible and fit running into the rest of my day instead. It gave a real boost to my morale. Don't do things at a time someone else dictates but at a time that feels good to you. I still prefer to run at the beginning of the day as it's over and done with then, and there is no opportunity for me to talk myself out of it later.

My sofa is comfortable, my living room is warm, and I am happy sat there with my gadgets, but sat there playing with toys will never give me the buzz that I get when I finish a run. It won't do anything for my waistline either; in fact, sat there I would be more tempted to eat junk food. At least if I go out and run I can earn that chocolate treat without feeling guilty.

So instead of coming up with an excuse why you can't run, pull on those trainers, get out that door and tell me that it doesn't feel better!

LESSON: It's easy to come up with an excuse but feels much better when you don't.

Pickering 10k October 2008

This turned out to be a non-starter as I was still suffering from shin splints from the Castle Howard 10k and was coming down with a cold.

However, I headed off to the gym and managed to do 10k on the treadmill instead!

First 5k in 26:25 and the full 10k in 56:04

I was a very happy bunny with those times I can tell you. That said I'm not sure I could have done the distance in the cold.

LESSON: Listen to your body, don't run if you're ill.

I ran FIVE miles

2nd November 2008 - probably means nothing to you but it's the first time I ever ran five miles without stopping!

It was cold, it was drizzling with rain, it was windy, and I couldn't breathe thanks to a cold but I did it - yahay!

Sadly, I didn't get the reception I expected when I got home, I honestly don't think they understood just how big a deal this was for me, so I rang my little brother and got the 'well done' that I'd been looking for.

LESSON: When these milestones happen, make sure you have someone you can ring who will understand how important they are to you.

Thirsk 10 November 2008

What can I say but never, ever, ever, again. Not only was it a nightmare due to injury, but it was freezing! Literally! We were running on sheet ice in places, but that seemed to be the least of the problems.

I'd managed 37 miles of run/walking so far that month, in fact the previous week had been my longest run yet at 7.57 miles in 1:37:35 on deep but fresh laid snow, leading me to believe I could hit my target of 1:45 on race day.

I suppose the fact I had been ill most of the preceding week, I hadn't run since the previous weekend when I struggled with 7 1/2 miles in the snow, and I'd put myself under too much pressure over this race were all contributing factors to the disaster that was about to unfold.

Kate arrived at my house that morning, all bright and breezy as usual, to give me a lift and to run with me.

We arrived at Thirsk with an hour and a half to spare and realised just how cold it was, but we huddled up in the lobby and met up with several of our running friends.

It was freezing everywhere, the toilets where we were changing were outdoors and draughty, there were people wearing bin bags to keep them warm and I was surrounded by 'proper' runners. (translate that as people who knew what they were doing and mainly belonged to a club). It was good to meet up with several other Fetchies, but I knew I would end up running alone.

It was a long walk to the start and suddenly we were off, well the rest of them were, I settled into my steady pace as everyone else shot off into the distance. I was coping with a nice steady 9:30/10:30 pace and knew, as always, that I would find the first two miles the hardest. I completed those two miles and realised that I had now run over 200 miles since June - not bad for someone who had spent the last sixteen years on the sofa!

Before we completed those first two miles at least six club runners had dropped out. I just kept telling myself I would be fine, mile one was a tenth of the way, mile two was a fifth of the way and if nothing else I'd beaten those club runners!

You've got to understand that the village where I live is flat, a kerb is classed as a hill round here, and, despite Thirsk being classed as a flat course, I have never seen so many hills! Okay, they may have been short in stature but they went on and on and on and were all steady climbs. I would say that miles three to five were all hill, or at least felt like it.

I also found that having spent weeks hoping I would have someone to follow it was harder than I thought. The person in front of me was run/walking, and every time she slowed to walk my body ached to walk as well. I kept teasing myself that I'd walk in another mile, get there and tell myself I could manage yet another mile before I walked and I knew I could manage seven miles of running as I had done it in training.

As soon as I hit the main road I lost all my confidence, I'd never run on a road with so much traffic before. I had my iPod on low so I could hear the traffic but I might as well have not bothered. Drivers were obviously frustrated and instead of waiting for a car to pass they tried to pass us two cars at a time. A couple of runners ahead of me nearly collapsed on the verge having been forced there by a lorry that refused to give way.

Around mile 5 came the water stop... that's when I slowed down to take on some water and everything went horribly wrong. Suddenly my left hip hurt like hell and I can't say my right knee was doing too well either. It was the slowing down that seemed to make it so noticeable and I suspect it was the camber of the road and the hills that caused the damage. Bearing in mind at this point I had passed the water station, no runners were to be seen in front of me and I could at best hobble rather than run. I was also in the middle of God knows where and had no idea of how to get back so decided I was going to do this. That northern grit kicked in and I limped along, bawling at the pain and frustration and just kept going. I also didn't want to give anyone the satisfaction of saying 'I told you so' if I couldn't finish.

Then comes the switchback, I hate and detest switchbacks. If you're a back of the pack runner like me (I seem to have a habit of last but one finishes) then you see the lead runners coming back towards you and know you have a shed load of pain and distance ahead of you still before you can get back to this point. What I hadn't realised was that I also had to run past a chicken farm, and trust me, there is no worse smell on a frosty wintery morning than that, especially when you have to go past slowly due to the injury. On the way back I have no idea how I didn't break my neck on the sheet black ice that covered 75% of the road, the main problem being the other 25% of the road was being occupied by fast moving vehicles.

With about two miles still to go I thought I must have taken a wrong turn as a runner was running towards me. Nope, I was heading the right way, it was one of my amazing Fetch buddies, Mel, come back after finishing their race to keep me company and help me finish. Then another Fetch buddy, Helen, arrived to take over. What can I say about the spirit these guys show? It makes so much difference, and unless you are one of the back of the pack finishers who is used to everyone having gone home by the time you finish, I don't think you can ever understand it.

We finally came in sight of the race course and the traffic piling out looked just like a car boot sale finish. But these weren't car booters, they were runners. And they weren't stopping. I had my running number clearly displayed on my vest, and they expected me to stop running so they could let these cars out. My friend actually landed on the bonnet of one of them who refused to give way. I was horrified. Obviously not all runners have as much respect for each other as I thought.

We finally approached the entrance to the racecourse for the finish and there was one runner ahead of me, no one behind. I recall sobbing that I wouldn't be last but one and the really nice man in front of me saw the state of me and let me pass. It sounds really silly but finishing last really would have been the worst thing for me. I finished, injured, in a very, very, slow time of 2:08:02.

Luckily I had friends who had waited inside in the warmth for me and supplied me with hot tea and cakes. If I told you the car thermometer on the way back to York was still showing a minus figure at past 1pm you will understand just how cold a day it was.

Whilst I know there are races I have struggled with and need to race again to overcome those demons, I don't think I could ever face this nightmare again. It wasn't just the unpleasant route, the injury or the cold, it was the sheer lack of respect shown by the people who had finished ahead of me that upset me the most. To be truthful, if I hadn't had races booked already for the following year there is no way I would have pulled my running shoes on again it was that bad.

LESSON: I know some amazing runners but sometimes the odd one or two can be so very ignorant

RESULT: 10 Miles, 2:08:02 and one very disillusioned Helen

Edinburgh Marathon Hairy Haggis Relay May 2009

What an experience! I chose the 'Glory Leg' of the relay which is the 4.7mile last leg which meant I would get to cross a Marathon finish line. Well, it was my team and I was the most inexperienced runner in it. I also believed at this point that it would be the only marathon finish I would ever cross.

As it had been my 40th birthday just a few days before, we had decided to make a weekend of it in Edinburgh and chose a rather fine hotel to stay in, not realising just how close to the start we would be. Mind you it was at the top of a hill!

We managed to see a lot of our Fetch friends at the start, several of whom we had shared a pasta and pizza with the previous evening, then it was time to go catch the relay buses and say goodbye to husband and child for several hours.

The buses weren't working as well as they should; in fact our second leg runner had to catch a regular bus and had no change on her (a kindly fellow passenger paid her fare for her) almost missing her changeover. The third leg runner and I were on the same bus as each other as we had the same changeover point.

We were literally right on the coast and that day there was a heat wave. The first problem we encountered was trying not to get run over crossing the road to our start point, firstly because of the number of buses dropping off in our lane, and then trying not to get in the way of the runners going in the opposite direction in the other lane. Yes, we had to cross two lanes to get to the changeover and both were full of either vehicular or human traffic. I am amazed that no one was hurt to my knowledge.

It was a beautiful day to watch a race if you were a spectator, sadly not so beautiful a day if you were trying to run it. The leg before mine was around 8 miles long, and they had no water left at the water station because some thieving bugger had stolen it the previous evening, and despite the heat wave being predicted, they hadn't been able to get through the traffic to replace it. Needless to say our leg three runner had a very hard time of it.

But now the wait was over and it was my turn to run, I'd twisted my ankle on my run the previous weekend and had been limping on and off all week, but felt okay at the start. That is till I ran round the first bend which took me away from the coast and inland to a wall of heat. I nearly fell over!

As usual the flat course was full of what felt like hills to me but I managed a run/walk and was lucky to have a bottle of water with me. I couldn't quite grasp why the runners in front of me kept weaving from one side of the road to the other, and then I realised they were trying to catch what little shade there was available.

As I ran I saw several runners at the side of the road who had collapsed and were being treated by medical staff. It was quite scary but not surprising, considering the heat and what we later found out about the theft of the water.

One of the funniest things on route were the children with water guns being given permission by their parents to fire at the runners! They were obviously so used to be told 'no' that they couldn't quite believe it was okay to do it that day. Then there was the kindly soul who had his hosepipe out, watering the runners on the side of the road as we ran through that welcome but very brief shower of cold water.

I was tiring but kept myself going by looking at the people all around me who were running the marathon; if they could run a marathon in this heat then I sure as heck could manage just under five miles. I was just looking for a chance to walk and get my breath as soon as the spectators thinned when I realised it wasn't going to happen; spectators were crowded around the course now all the way to the finish line at the racecourse. That was a long and hard finish but the atmosphere was unbelievable. I was so used to finishing when everyone else had gone home that this support was overwhelming. People I didn't know were shouting my name (it was printed on my shirt) and encouraging me, and it gave me such a buzz. I found it very anti-climatic once I actually crossed the line though, there seemed to be a lot of confusion about where we should go as finishers, we couldn't find the meeting points and we were on the wrong side of the racecourse to the spectators.

Having finally found husband and child I realised they had missed my finish as the spectator buses had been late and they had arrived after me. Luckily they had met up with other members of my team and found a table at the coffee shop, and what a welcome cup of tea that was.

In hindsight we should have been better prepared for communicating with each other as a team as we didn't know when people had finished, what their times were, nor where we were meeting at the end but these were all little things.

That evening we went out for a meal and several of the marathon finishers were wearing their finishing t-shirts with pride. I left mine in the room as I felt that as just a runner in the relay it wasn't right, the glory belonged to those amazing people who ran a full marathon in that heat.

LESSON: Don't rely on supporters seeing you finish, it's much better if they can see you at one or more points on the course, it's much more motivating

RESULT: 4.7 miles Time: 54:10

Jane Tomlinson 10k York 2009

This was the first year that the Jane Tomlinson 10k would be taking place in York, so it felt like one of those races that you should enter.

I had decided I would not run in my normal running kit but in a multi coloured tutu and a black top. The logic was that the tutu would take the pressure off. If I was seen to be running in normal kit then people would expect me to do well, whereas the tutu would mean no one expected anything from me. It was a way of taking the pressure off.

I started the race with my friend Clare but soon realised I couldn't keep up with her steady pace. For me this was going to be a mix of running and walking in order to get round.

It was a packed course, and I found it awkward finding my own space and sticking to a sensible rhythm. It's far too easy to get caught up matching the speed of the runner in front of you when really you should be pacing yourself.

The route takes you into York on one side of the river, through town, which at that time on a Sunday morning only has the odd tourist who looks at you as though you're mad, and round by the Minster, before heading back through town and back down the other side of the river.

The Minster may be a nice touch but in all honesty you're there and gone in a matter of seconds so don't really get to appreciate it.

I suddenly realised I needed the bathroom but hadn't got any money on me, luckily someone who was just leaving left the door open for me, I was rather grateful.

The narrow path down back by the river was very challenging considering the number of runners trying to fit into the small space. As most of my runs were done around the village and alone I always found it hard to run in a group.

I started a walk break and got chatting to a lovely lady who was a nurse. We were keeping each other going. I'd been aiming for a PB (personal best time) but decided that helping this lady finish was more important. She'd recently been divorced and her family had told her she wouldn't be able to finish the race. This made me so cross. If your loved ones can't support you who can? We were both struggling a little when we reached the racecourse entrance but kept at it. It was so much nicer knowing I was helping someone else finish and realise their dream. I could aim for a PB another race, this felt more special. We crossed the finish line together and who'd have guessed it, I got that PB anyway.

I'm pretty sure it wasn't all me pulling her along, in fact I know that I probably wouldn't have done anywhere near as well trying to do it alone.

LESSON: Don't try and keep up with the pack, and if you can run with someone else it's always easier.

RESULT: 10k Time: 1:16:01

Back in the swing of it - July 2011

To set the scene, the last time I ran was in July 2010 when I made a total prat of myself at School sports day in the Mothers' Race by falling flat on my face several steps from the start. Needless to say I blamed the sodden grass as it had rained during the afternoon, and I limped off with a torn knee and damaged pride. Luckily my daughter wasn't embarrassed. I managed to limp my way, very slowly, to the finish line which is more than can be said of the two Dads who fell over in the Fathers' Race and sloped back off to their seats.

Before that I hadn't run since July 2009 when I did the first Jane Tomlinson 10k. As you can see that's a bit of a gap. I had however committed myself to the Jane Tomlinson 10k in July of this year that I had yet to start training for.

I'd arranged a work training weekend in Birmingham in mid June and one of my friends, Sarah, sent me a message to bring my running kit with me for the following morning. You can imagine the lack of joy that greeted the proposal at my end but hey, if she wanted to go running then off we would go.

The morning dawned damp and wet after a lot of rain the night before and my roommate hurried me up so I wasn't late then hid back under her duvet (so not fair) while I tramped wearily outside.

This was a very ad hoc affair; we were at the side of a motorway and with no idea where to run. We were next to the NEC so decided to use the truck car parks as our running route, much to the concern of my friend who is used to treadmill running, and there we were running over deep puddles and muddy car parks. Bearing in mind how long it was since I last ran and that my friend had never run outdoors, or for much more than a mile, we amazed ourselves by what we achieved.

The iPhone app was having trouble picking up a signal but we managed to work out that we ran just short of two miles in around 25 minutes. And the key word there is RAN. I ran without stopping. I'd not managed that for a long time; previously I had accepted that I was a run/walker. I think I was more than elated, the buzz was unbelievable, in fact I actually sprinted down the hotel corridor back to the room. (The Premier Inn carpet made it feel like I was floating!)

I had spent month after month believing I couldn't do it, putting it off because it might hurt, because it was cold, because it was too warm, you name it, I had an excuse. And the joke of it is, look at all that perfectly good running I missed out on.

Since then I managed several small runs, building up the mileage slowly so that hopefully I could run the Jane Tomlinson 10k without stopping I wasn't sure how do-able that would be but I was going to give it a damned good try!

LESSON: Stop coming up with excuses, you might just enjoy it.

Jane Tomlinson 10k York July 2011

This was the second Jane Tomlinson I'd done but it was the first where I set myself a target of running non-stop. I'd not raced since the Jane Tomlinson 10k in 2009, and then not run in over a year thanks to a combination of injury and lack of self-belief.

Just two months before the race I still hadn't started training. You know that idea you have in the back of the mind that you will start tomorrow? That was me.

Anyway, the training got kick started, thanks to that two mile run in Birmingham, and race day arrived, warm and sunny. For a 9am start it was a very warm day.

To say York is supposedly flat there was a slow but steady climb at the start and I seemed to be able to maintain the speed I wanted. However, I was so mid-pack that I was finding it hard to progress through the field in places, particularly down some of the narrower streets.

If you've previously been a run/walker then trying to run amongst run/walkers can be very frustrating, the temptation to walk when they walk is unbelievable, and to see them sprint past you when they are back in the run mode can be demoralising.

The route takes you past the Minster, and with the sun shining this was a beautiful view but you only see it for a minute or so before you're back in the city streets, then back down by the river.

This back section of the race is where it started to get hard. I knew my supporters were back in the city and no one was there for me at the finish (my choice as you never see them at the finish and the three sightings during the run had done me the world of good), and I was starting to tire. The hill (okay steep rise) was nearly the end of me, but sheer bliddy determination kept me going, through the race course car park and down the side of the stands entrance.

One of the run/walkers that had been haunting me for most of the route suddenly sprinted past me towards the home straight and I nearly stopped right there. I honestly didn't think I could make that last 300 yards or so at that point.

I was too hot, struggling, and had poured the best part of two bottles of water over my head to cool me down, and it still wasn't enough. But I did it, somehow, just taking it step by step, and crossed that finish line, making it the first 10k I had raced and run all the way and with a shiny new PB that I hadn't expected either 1:10:59 against the run/walk of 2009 1:16:01.

Of course the side effect of pouring two bottles of water over your head whilst running a 10k is that when you finish you suddenly realise you look like you've just got out of the shower! I squelched through the finish funnel, collected my t-shirt (I prefer medals) and handed in my chip, walking to the end of the street where my lift was waiting to take me home.

Before I'd even made it to the car my race time was texted through on my phone by the race organisers, a lovely touch and much earlier than expected.

So would I do this race again? It's expensive when you look at longer races, and not all the entry fee goes to charity but I think I would. It's a challenging route for me and I would love to come back another year and conquer those hills (I know they're really steep rises but they feel like hills to me!).

LESSON: Don't give in and walk because someone else is, stick to your guns

RESULT: Distance - 10k Time - 1:10:59

Slow but steady - August 2011

I was looking forward to a planned run as my brother had promised to join me, but he cried off.

I went anyway, knowing that I'd never get up to half marathon distance sitting on my butt after all. (I'd booked Brass Monkey half marathon for the coming January).

The sun was out which was very welcome after the previous day's torrential rain, but thanks to the rain it meant having to take the safe, dry, boring round the streets rather than my preferred scenic off road route.

I started off well enough at an average 10.30 pace but couldn't maintain it and found the last mile and a bit were over 12 pace. My leg didn't feel brilliant and I decided to not do the optional extra loop I'd considered.

2.35 miles in 27:56 felt slow but was my best solo pace to date. I just needed to get control of the pace going forward, I was far too up and down. It wasn't as fast as the previous week's 10k but I did have several thousand other runners there to help me maintain pace.

I found I wasn't enjoying the act of running right then, that hadn't come back yet, but I did love the feeling of accomplishment when I reached home, crashed out and realised I ran the whole thing.

I was happy to work at upping the distance rather than speeding up but wanted to be more consistent on pace, as it had been very demoralising to see it drop off so much.

It's a bit like dieting I guess, that has always worked better when I plan the week and stick to it so realised I needed to put runs in the calendar and get up and go.

Don't get me wrong, I was pleased with the fact I got out there and did the run, and it was over 2 miles, but as always I wanted more and wanted to up it to nearer 3 miles next time if I could.

LESSON: I have found that slowing it down allows me to go further, not every race is a sprint and if you want to increase your distance don't be afraid to slow it down.

Size 12 Jeans - August 2011

It may not sound like much but I could get in them again, and I had just treated myself to a new pair, the last time I could wear size 12 jeans was early 2008 and I had been in a size 16 that last Xmas so......get in!

This left me feeling rather chuffed and jolly. I still wasn't in size 12 trousers yet but leave that with me was my attitude.

LESSON: Not all successes are running related, celebrate each achievement along your journey.

I'm not quite waterproof - August 2011

I had decided to set myself more of a training plan than waking up on a morning, sticking my finger in the air and deciding if I would run or not. As it turned out the training plan I picked from Fetch Everyone had me running Tuesdays, Thursdays and Sundays which kind of fitted in if I could get my butt out of bed early enough to be back before my husband went to work, as my daughter wasn't yet at a stage where she could run with me and keep up and not peeve me off. She was too negative.

Knowing I would have her running at some point, she was all for joining me when it came to buying new trainers and a running top but as soon as I tried to get her out there her enthusiasm melted quicker than the ice cream she left out of the freezer.

Our darling weather decided to throw me a blinder and it was raining heavily when I woke up. I was going to call it off, but then realised that wouldn't get me anywhere and I have never actually minded running in the rain. One of my best runs had been in fresh fallen snow so bad weather doesn't bother me, although my worst run ever which nearly stopped me running for life, was that very ice covered Thirsk 10 mile run.

It was raining heavier than I had realised but I was fine, I had my shorts on and my running top and off I went. It felt quicker, I wasn't sure why, but it felt comfortable, okay it wasn't breaking any records but it wasn't as hard work as the previous Tuesday's run. Possibly because it was a lot cooler and as my running was mostly done over autumn/winter in the past I suspect this is what I was more comfortable with.

I could have done without the railway crossing going down as I approached, even slowing down I still had to stand around for a bit. I suspect I looked rather odd to anyone on the train, a wet bedraggled woman doing side steps and marching on the spot.

Even with that I beat the previous Tuesday's time, and I'd run further, it just felt so much better. Of course I looked like a drowned rat by the time I got home and my Garmin didn't look like it was particularly waterproof (it wasn't my friend anymore as it kept running out of battery, I much preferred the iPhone running app which talked to me from my back pocket, much to the amusement of passers-by).

My lovely squash everything flat sports bra actually felt like it weighed three or four times as much as when I'd put it on, and the running kit was a lot wetter going in the wash than when it came out, but I didn't care.

I enjoyed my run, it felt good, and that feel-good lasted all morning. It was heading back home from my clients in the pouring rain that brought me crashing back down to earth. Whilst I don't mind running in the rain, I heartily detest it any other time, especially when this was supposed to be summer. I think I blinked and missed summer, or was it that glorious couple of weekends back at Easter?

I was planning three miles for the coming Sunday. Depending on how I felt I thought I might even do more; I had a 5k coming up on the Tuesday night that I didn't particularly like as a course but wanted to beat my time from 2008 if I could. At least this time I knew I could run the whole thing rather than the run/walk of last time and would be happy just to achieve that.

I'd talked several of my Twitter buddies into having a bash at running, which was good, it's always nice to know I have inspired somebody out there.

And the best part is that, thanks to all that running, I was able to have the yummiest pudding with my tea and still not go over my points allowance on my diet. Little things like that make running so much more worthwhile.

LESSON: Don't be afraid to get wet when you run, after all, your skin is waterproof!

York Millennium Bridge 5K - August 2011

I did it!

The York Millennium Bridge 5k isn't one of my favourite races, in fact it's the first race I did when I started running back in 2008 (correction, run/walking).

I detest the loop round the lake twice and the Millennium Bridge crossing sends me dizzy.

Now that I'd finally got back out there after not running since 2009 it obviously was one of the things I had to do again. Just to show myself I could.

Safe to say it's not the most organised race I have ever been to and the cereal bar you get on finishing ranks rather low on my list of rewards, but it had to be done.

So how did it go this time out? I ran the whole thing. I had had enough at 3k which oddly is just when you finish the double loop. I seriously wanted to slap every single marshal who said 'you are doing well' during the double loop (they were lovely though), the bridge wasn't as wobbly as the 10k race last month, and I got beaten by an 81 year old.

But..... I ran the whole thing and I did it in 31:53 as opposed to 36:25 last time out. I also had about 10 other people behind me for a change when I finished rather than finishing last but one.

So that was a huge big fat scary demon conquered.

As for Thirsk......I think that's one demon that is best left undisturbed! I was booked in to tackle Sutton 10k the following month and was quite looking forward to it now.

LESSON: Sometimes it's good to go back and try again

RESULT: Distance - 5k Time - 31:53

Run Fat Girl Run

A lot of people wonder why I chose to call my running blog 'Run Fat Girl Run'. http://www.runfatgirlrun.co.uk

Obviously the main reason was my love of the film 'Run Fat Boy Run'.

'But you're not fat?' they'd say. To me I was. After having my daughter in 2002 I lost three stone. Over the next few years I gained that weight back.

I distinctly remember my very young daughter sharing a bath with me and asking me 'Mummy, why do you have three bellies?'. Okay, I'd gained a bit of a bulge. My previously flat stomach now had a wobble, and if I was honest with myself, did look like three bellies.

But it's more than that. Over the years I have gained and lost weight. It's not really the weight that bothers me as much as how I felt I looked, and how I felt in my clothes, and for a long time I hadn't felt good in my own skin.

I'd lost weight again, felt pretty good in two or three dresses that I own, but it wasn't just the look anymore.

In the film Dennis says the line 'but I'm not fat, I'm just unfit', and that was as much a part of the blog title as anything.

The blog came about at around the same time I started running again after yet another long break from it.

It's a kind of sarcastic blog title I guess, but it's there for me, it means something to me. More than being overweight, it's about getting my head in the right place as well.

I know people who weigh 8 stone wet, it doesn't mean they don't have days when they feel fat, they may not look fat to others, but that isn't the point. It's how you feel inside that matters, and that blog title and that phrase is what helps me feel good inside and reminds me of where I need to be.

LESSON: Don't get too caught up in measurements, how you feel is much more important.

I'm no longer alone - September 2011

Thanks to Twitter not only did I now have a local running buddy but one that ran at my pace as well!

We went on our first run and I planned for four miles which turned into 4.71 as we managed the Common and the River Bank as well with no need for the long curvy streets I dislike.

Sam had run a Marathon, albeit she says it was her first and last, and the GNR but had now declared herself a 10k runner which I could understand. I still felt the need to run one marathon just to prove something to myself but was hoping this horrible premonition about getting a place in the London ballot was wrong as I wasn't ready for that level of training yet. Mind you seeing as the best I could pick at York races was one third place winner I was hoping I might be okay.

What was more immediately concerning was that Sam kept saying I needed hill training! Whilst she may have been right the prospect was not filling me with glee right then. Rumour has it there would be a hill involved the following week when it was her turn to choose the route, and she also mentioned a session just of hill reps. If I hadn't already signed up for races, now would have been a good time to consider quitting!

I still couldn't say I enjoyed running yet but I bloody loved finishing! That buzz sets you up for the day. I did feel like a puffer train running behind Sam at one point as I was doing a heck of a lot of puffing, but eventually I almost found it comfortable. As the route was mainly off road I wasn't disappointed at the pace and was happy to be able to run without stopping which was a huge improvement on the year before last.

It was so good to run with someone who was a similar age, does a similar job, and who knows what I'm on about when I talk running. Very refreshing. If she would stop using the hill word (notice how that's a four letter word!) I would be very happy to run with her again.

LESSON: It's great to run with someone else if they run at the same pace as you.

Sutton Park 10k September 2011

My first and only attempt at this was back in 2008 as a 7 mile race, when my run/walk earned me a finish time of 1:27:25 and a sore ankle from the rather large rubble on the airfield surface.

This year it was a 10k race (although my running app only clocked it as 6.07 miles but that could have been a weak GPS signal) and the route had altered from country road and airfield to off road, tiny bit of country road, and airfield.

We set off from the playing field, through the village and into the grounds of Sutton Park, across a patch of damp slippery grass and into the woods. Now whilst the woods is a terrain I am lucky enough to regularly train on, it is also a terrain where I am traditionally about a minute a mile slower than on tarmac, and coupled with the fact the trail was narrow in places, making it hard to find suitable overtaking points, I wasn't holding out much hope of a good time from the start. I thought painting the tree roots in the path bright green was a nice idea so we could see them, but I did manage a couple of twists on my ankle from the uneven surface anyway.

Round one field, over another field of stubble, through a very narrow nettle lined gap between trees, and then over a bare earth field (boy was I glad it wasn't raining) before hitting a narrow country lane where we met the race leaders heading back and two lanes of traffic trying to compete with runners in either direction.

There's something quite demoralising about seeing the lead runners head off in the opposite direction to you and knowing you have a hell of a lot of running to do to get back to this point. There was a water station on the entrance to the airfield and most of that went over my head to cool me down, (note to self, the zip up running top does not work well if you pour water over your head, the collar becomes very heavy and annoying!)

Looking back on the photos, runners 34 and 35 had been just behind me at the start and entered the airfield just behind me, after the water station I started running with them, more to do with the fact I really didn't have enough puff left to get back ahead of them again! The airfield is a huge loop and a large portion of the race. It's a cracked, crater-filled concrete path that seems to go on forever, but at least this year most of the rubble appeared to have been removed which my ankles were most grateful for. At one point you run through a pig farm, right next to the pig sheds, which aside from the rather off-putting squealing, (which I chose to interpret as 'shift your backside') I can only say was enough to clear the sinuses no matter how bad your cold was.

We got back on to the country lane at about the 8k mark and there was a long country lane in front of us. I honestly think the giant loop of the air field was less daunting. At the entrance to the airfield there was another water station, but I managed to spill more of the water down my front than I managed to drink! Plastic cups are not runner friendly, but the children manning the water stations were doing a fantastic job.

The 9k marker appeared at about the same time I really felt I had run out of run. Luckily runners 34 and 35 were two lovely ladies who encouraged me along and kept checking to make sure I was still with them. It was hard work by this time which did make me wonder how on earth I could be thinking of entering half marathons the next year if I struggled at 10k distance but I dug in, and managed to cross the line in 1:06:37 which was a huge shiny new PB for me, and even more special thanks to the terrain and the cold and dodgy knee I was suffering with.

Having looked back at the splits I was really pleased with the lap times. I'd recently decided not to run with a Garmin and worry about lap times or pace as I found the watch uncomfortable and monitoring the pace distracting. I tried instead to just maintain a comfortable pace and see what happened. I would rather complete the distance than worry about the speed.

Needless to say I was delighted with my time though felt rather rough when I had finished. The race memento that year was a choice between an engraved tumbler or an engraved coaster, I chose the coaster and it's one of my favourite mementos from running. I think I probably pushed myself too hard on this one and whilst my legs didn't feel too bad after all the stretching the same could not be said of my stomach and chest which felt like they had been hit by a truck the following morning and were very uncomfortable all evening.

With nearly a month to my next 10k, the Woodland Challenge in Huddersfield, I confess to wondering if I would ever progress beyond this distance, or run it comfortably. In the meantime I would carry on running off road and include some hill work in preparation for that and the Dalby Dash in November.

The following month would signal whether I had a place in the Virgin London Marathon or not. I was praying not right then, and wondering whether I would need to join a local running club, rather than just running for my online club. My husband had been chatting to some of the marshals at Sutton and their advice if I wanted to do distance running was to join a club. It's something I needed to give serious thought to over the next few weeks. Running with a buddy had already made a big difference but I was conscious that I needed to really learn techniques and running style if I was going to make anything of my running.

Overall I was very pleased with my performance, I ran the whole thing which was the main target for me this time out, the knee held up really well with the knee support, and I'd achieved my best time yet for this distance. It made a huge difference finishing the race before everyone had gone home, and knowing there were still a few runners behind me.

There are nicer routes to race but this race was about beating demons from my last time here, and I had succeeded at that. As for whether I would choose to race this course again I wasn't sure, I suspect I would be more likely to look at a more scenic route for my October runs such as Thornton Le Clay which was happening the following week.

LESSON: Never pour water over your head when you're wearing a zip top running top, it gets heavy and uncomfortable!

An evening with Caballo Blanco - September 2011

It's not often you get an opportunity to meet a legend, especially from the world of Ultra Running, but having recently read 'Born to Run.' I couldn't pass up an evening with Caballo Blanco. He was very tall and lean and with his shaved head was not quite what I was expecting; where was the hippy hermit from the book?

He wasn't a natural speaker but did an excellent job of keeping the audience entertained and there were plenty of moments where he had us all laughing.

This wasn't the man from the book, he was actually very at ease with people, he communicated well, and whilst he was reluctant to be in the spotlight, his passion for the Tarahumara and for running shone through. Despite having done several of these events over the past few weeks around the world he still appeared nervous about being the centre of attention, sipping on water all evening, but the first thing he did was kick off his lightweight shoes and spend the rest of the evening talking to us in his socks.

He shared with us his early running history, and how he came to be acting as pace runner for the Tarahumara in that fateful Leadville 100. His stories are full of humour, yet have a serious message. It wasn't until the Q&A section at the end that he even mentioned technique. His advice was to run light, and enjoy it, and not worry about what you wear, he was neither for nor against various running shoes, and only commented that he found running in sandals helped him develop his running style and cut down on injury. How ironic that he had tried running in London recently and ended up injured.

Having read the book I did wonder why Caballo Blanco was here, this man who didn't like the spotlight, didn't want sponsorship and loved the peace and tranquillity of the Canyon. What could persuade him to travel half way round the world to talk to us? All became clear. He had set up a non-profit to help the Tarahumara people, to give them back the means to grow their own crops, to sponsor the races between the villages, to help them be able to continue to run. To hear him talk about the Tarahumara was wonderful, he really cared about this community, and it was good to see that, as in the book, he had avoided the lure of corporate sponsorship, and was keen to avoid the so called offers of support that were thinly veiled attempts at cashing in on the Tarahumara name.

Caballo was extremely generous with his time, having already confessed at the start of the evening to being tired as a result of his gruelling travel and speaking schedule, and signed copies of the book and posed for photos with most of the room who gave him a standing ovation after his talk.

It was inspiring to listen to him talk about running, and especially ultra-running, his passion and enthusiasm shone through, and whilst I didn't expect I would ever work my way up to taking part in the Copper Canyon Ultra, I would love to visit just to meet these people he speaks with such affection about. The way the community spirit around the Copper Canyon has grown is amazing. What started as a small race some six races before the one we read about in the book has grown to include an international field of runners, a race which generates a year's income for the community in just one week every year.

I was moved by this quiet and gentle man; he talked a lot of sense, had some very good rules to live his life by, and was very inspiring. I am so glad that I got the opportunity to listen to him, and very honoured that I got to have my photo taken with him.

I was so saddened to hear of his death in early 2012. It made that rare opportunity to meet him even more special.

This evening was also the first time I met a couple of the runners from the York Postal Harriers, a local running club. They left me thinking really hard about whether I wanted to join a 'proper' club. It was something I would need to look at.

LESSON: Running can introduce you to some of the most amazing people you will ever meet.

Treadmill v Outdoor Running

A lot of people have never experienced running other than on the treadmill in the gym, and I feel sorry for them, because there is a whole lot more to running outdoors that they will miss out on.

I get that there are some benefits to running on a treadmill, and that there are times when it's the only option, but I would encourage anyone who has only ever run on a treadmill to give it a go outdoors.

On a treadmill you never go anywhere, which is handy if you've had enough because you can just stop and you are still at the gym; it's a disadvantage out on the road if you need to stop miles from home, but it's also an encouragement to keep going. If you've still got to get home you may as well run it.

On a treadmill you don't feel the rain, the wind or the sun. Trust me, I've run in wind, rain and snow as well as sun and you cannot beat the experience, it adds to the feeling, and is a much more rewarding challenge.

On a recent morning's run I'd seen a shower of leaves falling from the trees, the various warm autumnal colours, I ran along a trail, full of colour, smells and occasionally wildlife; you don't get that on a treadmill. But the upside with a treadmill is that you do get to watch TV!

Running on a treadmill you don't get the camaraderie that you get when running outdoors. In my village, most people I pass when running smile and say hello and it encourages you; mind you they often also give me a look of sympathy as well, so I imagine it's not a pretty sight!

Changing your route when you run outdoors makes it feel like a different run every time. One of the best runs I ever had was along the side of the beach in Salou. It was the most amazing view, the sun was rising, everything was clean and peaceful, and it was great. Granted returning to the village runs where the view is wood, trees and slugs wasn't quite the same but it's still a lot more scenic than the treadmill.

Running outdoors is free! I know I am not the only one who's signed up to a gym with the best intentions and then never gone, wasting the monthly membership. Running outdoors I don't have to worry about the cost, what the opening hours are (outdoors is open 24/7) or what day of the week it is and how busy it will be.

So which camp do you fall into? The outdoor runner or the treadmill runner, or do you have a mix of both?

LESSON: Running on a treadmill is nothing like running outdoors, you really should experience outdoor running.

The frustration of not running

I am sure many runners will identify with the frustration of not running. Sometimes it's down to injury, sometimes ill health, or sometimes your diary conspires against you.

But have you ever noticed how many people seem to be running when you can't? It's as though these other runners multiply on a daily basis the longer you are unable to run.

Now given that on any day I have planned to run I am reluctant to head out of the door for those first few steps, it's amazing how much I want to run when I can't.

I'd had a sinus infection and hadn't run a step since the Sutton 10k the other week, in fact for over a week I hadn't even walked to school on a morning as I just didn't have the energy.

I walked to school finally and cannot tell you how good that fresh air felt, or how bad it felt because it took me twice as long as normal. Judging by the ache in my legs later on that morning you would have thought I'd run a good ten miles, not strolled a couple of miles instead.

During this period of enforced non-running I had been more involved with other runners than ever before, just to rub it in. Not only was I surrounded by runners but these guys were running half marathons and full marathons and the like, which obviously led to me saying that yes I would run a marathon in a year's time.

I don't think at the time I really meant it though!

LESSON: When you can't run and it looks like everyone else can, try not to let it get you down; instead concentrate on getting fit and getting back out there.

Knowing when to say no

One of the hardest decisions you have to make as a runner is when not to run.

Your natural inclination is to run come what may, but there are times when it doesn't make sense to do so. Sometimes, you have to listen to your body or take other factors into account before you make the decision.

I'd been ill for over a month, but I'd also been adamant I would run the Woodland Challenge 10k that weekend. I'd had a month of unbelievable stress due to the poor health of a family member, and until a few days earlier hadn't run a step since the Sutton 10k the previous month.

My husband advised me against running that weekend having seen what he calls 'the state of you' when I got in from my 3.5 mile run the previous Sunday morning. Okay I admit I did look a mess and out of breath but I'd run well; maybe didn't feel that good during the run but when I saw the splits I was a happy if shattered little bunny!

What with one thing and another I hadn't managed to get a second run in until later that week. For my own peace of mind I like to have a 5 mile run under my belt the week before a 10k; you can always pull off that extra mile if pushed during race conditions, but this particular morning fell just short of 3.5 miles. To hit the 3.5 meant running past my front door but once I saw home that was it, I'd had enough.

Whilst it was a good, if hard, run I knew that I couldn't have managed six miles, and that was the problem. To take part on the Sunday would have been too much. Even if by some miracle I managed to complete the distance, I suspect the toll on my health over the coming weeks would have been too much. I had goals for my running the following year that included half marathons and possibly a full marathon. Running more than I felt comfortable with, risking my health and injury, would put those goals in jeopardy. It wasn't worth it.

Why is it though that it's always the races you've really looked forward to that are the ones you have to pull out of. Someone called it sods law, I guess they are right.

LESSON: Sometimes saying no is the right decision.

Dalby Dash 10k 13th November 2011

For a race that I had been worrying about for some time, and nearly dropped out of just a couple of days before, this went surprisingly well. The day dawned damp and misty and didn't really improve on that, although I am told that it was considerably warmer than the same time the previous year.

The event takes place in Dalby Forest and the organisers are very honest about the hill at the start, 1 1/2 miles of uphill, which considering many of the flat races I have previously entered have felt hilly, meant that this was an official hill race. This obviously meant hard work.

I'd heard of Dalby Forest, yet despite it being only 40 minutes away had never been - it's very popular with mountain bikers and I can see why.

We arrived to find the tree tops covered in a blanket of mist, in fact it was misty everywhere. It's one of those races where most of the entrants are wearing club tops and is a 'proper' race. After all why would anyone in their right mind choose to run 10k up a steep hill for fun on a misty Sunday morning!

The race organisers were raising funds for Help for Heroes and a local charity, and just before 11am gathered us all together to listen to some Remembrance Day poetry before we all observed the 2 minutes' silence. What an awesome place to be for this I have to say, surrounded by beautiful hills, trees and the mist.

We were off, Sam (my running buddy who talked me into this particular race) and I were pretty much at the back from the start, deliberately. There are actually prizes for the fastest runners up the hill and we didn't want to get in anyone's way.

Ouch! I don't run hills and boy could my ankles tell. They were burning within seconds of setting off but I was stubbornly determined to run the hill if at all possible. I dug in and put my head down, thinking it would be easier than looking at this never ending hill up ahead of me and it kind of was, apart from the pain in my ankles. The poor things just aren't used to hills and were really struggling. I was only managing to run slowly, in fact some of the people walking the hill were keeping pace with me but I wanted to run as much of it as I could.

At the 2k mark, knowing that there was over another 1k of hill I gave in and walked a little only to find that actually hurt more! I couldn't get a rhythm on my breathing enough to carry on running so just did a fast walk for the next 1k and at the 3k mark we started running again. The brow of the hill was a very welcome sight but that then meant running down hill along a very muddy track, luckily this wasn't too long a stretch as I didn't feel safe for any part of it, convinced I was going to lose my footing on the steep descent and make a complete and utter fool of myself by falling head first (yep, I still hadn't got over the fall at Sports Day a couple of years ago!).

The track levelled out into rocky track, and as we were the only ones to be seen at this point it felt more like we were having a Sunday morning run on the common rather than taking part in a race. I have to say we both felt really comfortable throughout this stage, and from about 4k to 8.5k we were really enjoying it and surprised by how well we were running and how fresh we both felt, having a good laugh with the many mountain bikers heading uphill in the opposite direction.

At 8.5k the ascent starts again and that ease was gone. It was hard work to the finish now, with the last few hundred yards seeing the closest to a sprint finish we could manage.

For a race I was going to back out of, as I didn't think I was fit enough, I am so glad that I took part. The hill was bloody hard work and worse than I had anticipated, but all that meant was I was now determined to include some hill training in my workouts going forward. I did enjoy it and will probably have a go again another year and hopefully conquer that hill.

LESSON: Sometimes the races you dread the most turn out to be the best experiences instead.

RESULT: Distance - 10k Time - 1:09:17

I joined a running club - November 2011

I'd had a pretty good week in terms of running stuff for me. I'd had gait analysis re-done one afternoon by a local specialist running shop with very interesting results - my legs were different (now why does that not surprise me!). My right leg (the one with the previously torn ankle and knee) was perfectly neutral, the left leg however pronates! Now did you really expect me to conform? The gait analysis was really interesting, we started off in Asics GT2160 which was my current shoe (stability) then moved onto a neutral shoe and finally onto an Asics Gel 1160 model. (mild stability). All three attempts were videoed and compared side by side, leading to the conclusion that the 1160 was the better shoe all round. It was explained so clearly to me, including how each shoe worked; definitely an experience I would recommend.

The new shoes were a Christmas gift, which would give me just enough time to get comfortable in them before my first half marathon, Brass Monkey, in the coming January.

Of course, while I was there I had to check out the rest of the shop and was getting some new running kit for Christmas as well. It had to be done! I stuck with Ronhill, it appears that most of my kit is from them anyway, it's comfortable to wear and not as tight-fitting as some of the more sporty brands out there. It was bright pink so everyone would definitely see me coming!

I handed in my form and was now officially signed up to a local running club. I've always had a bit of a block about joining a club, preferring to be a member of an online group instead, until now. I realised that in order to progress my running from 10k to half marathon, and hopefully full marathon, I needed more support and encouragement than I get trying to do it alone.

I had several local clubs to choose from but opted for the York Postal Harriers. The guys I had met at the Caballo Blanco evening had invited me along for a taster session and I found the whole group light-hearted and easy to get on with, but also a great mixed group, slower runners were welcomed whilst there seemed to be a fair number of marathon runners as well. There was a lot of banter which I really enjoyed.

The weekly club run isn't just a run, it's a social thing as well as we all end up in the pub afterwards. It's fun, it's safer than running alone, and it's a good experience. Whilst they had this great light-hearted feel they were also serious about running.

I chose the shorter of the available routes, and at a slower pace than I would normally run. We ran just short of four miles and I really enjoyed it. I knew that running alone I have this tendency to go off too fast, and whilst I can just about complete a run, there was no fun in it, whereas on this occasion I enjoyed running.

That weekend I had Sam (my running buddy) joining me for around six or seven miles around the village as she helped me increase the distance over the next few weeks ready for Brass Monkey.

If I could slow it down a little I had no doubt I could do the distances, although I was reluctant to go down the heart rate monitor route to measure this as it just felt too technical, and running should be about fun shouldn't it?

I was still on a high from completing the Dalby Dash course the previous weekend and as a result was much more positive about my running.

LESSON: You don't have to join a running club but it can make a huge difference to your progress. However, do the research and make sure you find a club that is the right match for you.

Who'd have guessed I would enjoy running! - November 2011

I'd had a bit of an epiphany in my running over the past couple of weeks that I certainly hadn't been expecting. I'd started to really enjoy the act of running, rather than just the finishing. I knew it was bound to happen, how else could there be so many enthusiastic and happy runners out there? I just hadn't expected it to happen yet.

The first time it happened was at about the halfway mark at the Dalby Dash the other weekend. We were running well, we had energy left and the scenery was beautiful. The second time it happened was that Saturday; we had chosen half a route we knew and made up the rest, intending to hit the 7 mile mark if we could.

We started off in the village, getting the street element of it out of the way first, and headed off into the woods. The colours were amazing even if the roots were a bit tricky and just tempting me to fall flat on my face, but I beat them! However the same couldn't be said of the hidden muddy puddle. Sam jumped easily over the obvious muddy patch, but no, I had to be clever and try and go down the side that looked drier and easier, only to find myself in a puddle deeper than my trainer! I could feel the water seeping in, served me right.

It had started off as a very misty morning, and the hope was that by the time we made the main road the mist would have lifted enough for us to feel safe running on the road. The woods were very damp and wet but still colourful, although sadly rather lacking in wildlife. The main road runs between the common and the fields and has a couple of interesting cattle grids to negotiate, as well as being winding and pathless. The funniest part was watching the approaching tractor move all the way across the road to give us room, not something you often see, and I was pretty sure that after losing all that weight I wasn't that wide a load anymore - perhaps he was just trying to avoid my rather luminous pink kit.

I should explain, I do not have a pink fetish, despite my phone cover being pink at the time, as well as most of my running kit. It's down to practicality. To be visible when running during winter requires bright clothing which comes in pink or yellow. I don't like yellow. My phone was bright pink so that when I drop it in my bag instead of putting it in the special pocket I can find it again! The men reading this won't have a clue what that means but trust me, any gal who has the handbag with a black lining, that has everything bar the kitchen sink in it, will understand not being able to find your phone even when its ringing.

But I digress. We were on the last part of our run home and again having that 'I'm enjoying this running lark' feeling. Sam spotted a Marsh Tit (grey bird with black head to me) and then I spotted my robin. He's a lovely little chap, he plays tag with me when I run on the common and I hadn't seen him for months, so it made me very happy to see him again.

We resisted the urge to check out the running app until we had to make a route direction decision. We wanted to do seven miles and needed to know if an extra loop was required. We were delighted to know we had nearly cracked it. Oddly enough, it's always at the point that we check the running app that we discover we're feeling tired. All the more reason for it to stay safely tucked away in my back pocket till we've finished.

So the end result was 7.42 miles. Those 0.42 miles are incredibly important, because they made this the furthest I had ever run without stopping. So on top of the high you get from a satisfying run was the extra high of having achieved something new!

Running club that week was set to be a lovely steady run, somewhere between four and six miles depending on who was running where. Unfortunately our group was split up by an accident that happened at the same time we set off and I found myself keeping up with a couple of the faster runners. Not wanting to hold them back I dug in and stayed behind them, despite them dragging me up small hills! It was harder than I had planned, and faster, but you know what - I was so glad I had done it when I had finished.

The answer then to me was run slower. Take my time, enjoy the route and stop trying to compete against a clock or myself, and run at a speed where I can maintain a conversation instead of the speed where I feel like I cannot manage more than 'yeah' when asked if I am okay.

As I planned to increase my mileage over the next few weeks to prepare for my first Half Marathon I knew I would rather run slower and enjoy the journey than kill myself during the process. I was looking forward to my next run on the coming

Saturday morning, a steady eight miles and another new route to me. Bring it on!

Lesson: Your lovely new shiny white trainers will get dirty, don't sweat it, just appreciate that once they are muddy and black it's down to all the hard work and mileage you've put in.

parkrun January 2012

If you've never heard of parkrun it's a brilliant idea. It's a Saturday morning 5k run at venues around the UK. It's free to enter, although you must register on their website (www.parkrun.org.uk) at least the day before your first event to obtain your barcode, and then when you have your barcode you can turn up as and when you want at any event around the country.

The event is staffed by volunteers, and they'd like you to volunteer if you can several times a year. It's great to volunteer if you can't run due to injury or you can't run on a Saturday because it doesn't fit in with your training plan.

Because the event is free, and staffed by runners who have given up their time, it's a great atmosphere. I've seen people running with babies in buggies, young children taking part (who always beat me!) and whole families take part.

There's no pressure at all. Yes the front of the pack will finish in 16 minutes or so, but the team will still be there to cheer on the back of the pack runner who takes 45 minutes as well.

It's suitable for all ages and all levels.

What I like about parkrun is that it's not only a great way to test out your 5k skills but it's a good introduction to racing.

I would always recommend that you try a 5k parkrun before you enter or compete in your first 5k race.

For many runners like me who run alone, this is the first introduction to running with others of differing abilities.

Because they always seem to have such a friendly atmosphere it's a great place to introduce your children to running.

It's also somewhere you can turn up when you feel like it, no booking, no planning required.

I've seen people travel from all over to attend our local parkrun, but York does have a reputation as a fast and flat course, and we do have Poppy Coffee who bring their coffee van to warm us all up after the event.

Our parkrun is on York Knavesmire, my least favourite place to run and is one and a half laps. You just finish the first half lap when you cross the finish line for the first time, which was quite handy for my daughter when she sprained her ankle on her first ever parkrun. She could stop there and wait for me while I completed the course and I knew she was being well looked after by the volunteers and spectators, as well as being in my line of sight the whole way round.

Some parkruns hold special events such as running in your PJ's, dressing up as a character from Star Wars or some other theme, but it doesn't matter if you just want to turn up and run in your jogging suit.

It's so informal and yet so well organised, you receive a text telling you your official finish time and your finish position, and you get a free t-shirt when you've completed 10, 50 or 100 parkruns.

If you're nervous about running one, why not register anyway and offer your services as a volunteer for a couple of weeks until you get to know some of the other runners and feel more comfortable about the whole thing.

LESSON: If you're not yet ready to enter a race have a go at parkrun or just volunteer - it's a great friendly introduction to group running.

Running isn't all about your legs - January 2012

Having spent most of December 'on the bench', due to a virus, I'd recently managed a Boxing Day run followed by a New Year run. It was something I needed to do to get my head back in the right place. It struck me whilst out running that physical fitness isn't all that comes to bear when running, it's just a part of it, and a great part of it that we don't normally consider is the mental aspect.

When you have been ill or injured you get out of the habit, you find excuses to stop you going out, and you convince yourself that this is for the best.

When you're out running that little voice in your head is telling you that you can't do this, you should be home with your feet on the sofa.

We all know the hardest part of running is getting out of the door in the first place but I suspect getting your head in the right place trumps that.

Look at how you feel when you get that shiny new pair of trainers - they talk to you, begging you to take them out and get them dirty, to christen them. That's not your legs doing the talking is it?

So how do you overcome this hidden voice, this saboteur who insists on piping up at any opportunity?

For me it's sheer bloody mindedness, answering back and telling myself I can do this. It's a fine balance I am sure I have yet to learn, over when to run and when to rest when you are ill. I do know that you can make it worse by running when you shouldn't and possibly err on the side of caution too much, but I also know when I am giving in.

I set myself goals, I enter races so I have to get out the door. It's just something that works for me.

Running is a great time to think things through, or even not to think if that's what you need.

At this point time I no longer ran with earphones. It was something I had got into the habit of doing since I started entering races, but I did still run with music; my running playlist was on my phone and I used to play it through the phone speaker out of my back pocket. Some days if traffic was heavy I could hardly hear it, but better I hear the traffic and what was happening around me. On other days, quiet mornings, I could hear every word, not just the odd beat.

Running that morning was peaceful and quiet, there weren't many people out and about in the village so it was a morning where I could hear the tracks clearly. I played music I loved, that encouraged me to run. I heard my running app talk to me every mile, updating me on my progress, and I used that to keep going as well. I looked at what I'd accomplished, and broke it down into stages.

My last couple of runs had been just over three miles as I was still finding I was coughing a lot when running. I needed to up that again that weekend as my first Half Marathon was looming and it had a 2:45 cut off. I was sure that my running buddy

Cathy and I could achieve this, but suddenly being made aware of the cut off is disconcerting. 'The Voice' kicks in and starts trying to sabotage you, reminding you that it takes you two hours just to do 9.5 miles.

The last half of my last run was spent puddle dodging and working out the feasibility of a 2:45 cut off. Cathy had run a half marathon before. Granted it took her the time we were allowed, but the difference this time was we were running together. We could pull each other along. We'd done it before on training runs and we could do it again on race day. We just needed to keep to a 12 min mile pace. I knew we could do it, I believed in us, plus we all know we can do things on race day we didn't think possible previously.

So the most important part of my training this month was getting my head in the right place. Of course running played a part, but I had a stern talk with myself about getting my head in the right place, and being the stubborn northern lass that I am, I was pretty sure that I would make it. It wouldn't be from lack of trying I can tell you!

LESSON: If your head is in the right place you can accomplish anything; if it's not, you're setting yourself up for failure.

Brass Monkey Half Marathon - January 2012

What can I say, it was the day after my first attempt at a Half Marathon and I truly felt like I had been hit by a train. My hips were so sore and out of alignment that it wasn't funny, and I was waddling around like a drunken cowboy who's been in the saddle for weeks. But I didn't care 'cos I bleeding well did it!

That morning, after a rather sleepless night, I woke to pouring rain, but I wasn't overly concerned, I could run in the rain if needed but was happier if it stayed dry. The good news was the rain stayed away come race time, but unfortunately it was replaced by the most brutal wind I have ever known.

It never seemed to blow behind us, but was either so strong as a side wind it was actually forcing us aside or was straight ahead of us and felt like we were pushing against one of those American Football training machines that they physically push across the field.

Thanks to what was left of the lurgy I couldn't breathe through my nose, unless it was adjacent to the fields where the farmer had kindly recently deposited fresh slurry, and my face was on fire with sinus pain. In hindsight I probably wasn't fit enough to have run, all things considered, but once out there I couldn't stop. This could in part be down to my amazing running partner Cathy, who spent ten miles telling me I couldn't quit, that I could do this, and generally mentally dragging me along with her. She wouldn't give in.

The wind was so strong I couldn't even bawl my eyes out, much as I wanted to, the tears were stolen from me before they'd fully formed and I couldn't catch my breath long enough to bawl, although I did manage some rather choice swear words at the wind on occasion, leaving me with a rather sore throat that morning.

I think that as strong willed as I am I would have quit had it not been for Cathy. I remember thinking it was a good thing the marshal telling me we had hit the half way mark was on the other side of the road, because if he'd been on my side I would seriously have blacked his eye for him and his cheery message. Half-way wasn't something to celebrate, it meant I had the whole torture to endure yet again and by then I wasn't quite sure I had it in me. I did actually stop and think - no - I can't go on, till Cathy told me off - again!

I finally persuaded Cathy at mile ten that she should go ahead, I was at the point where I wasn't keeping up and it was going to damage her race time, which wasn't fair on her, and she was running really well. By this time my right ankle was sprained, my left foot hurt every time I put it down and both hips felt like they were in a vice. What a fun experience! I started to limp/walk and thought a short break from running would help. It felt like it hurt more to walk than to run, so I found a kind of limp/walk pace that kept me going, and certainly didn't lose me any ground against the run/walker ahead of me.

By this point there was no way I could quit. I'd limped further than that in the past, and for some reason, perhaps being on my own, the determination kicked in big time. I started a little mantra on the last hill, 'I can, I will', which helped me get up it anyway. I'm not sure what the passing motorists made of the mad Yorkshire lass talking to herself as she limped along the road though.

The only part of the whole experience I enjoyed was the look of pride on my Daughter's face as she hugged me at the finish. Oh and beating the time I thought it would take. However, she did later tell me she had asked my husband if that was me coming round the corner at the finish and he replied that no, it wasn't me but whoever it was didn't look very well at all. Guess that says it all!

I couldn't really tell you what the route was like, I'm sure many of the other runners found it attractive, I found it open and exposed and no matter where we went the wind fought against us. Yes it's a flat course apart from two bridges that cross roads and are fairly steep, to me anyway, but you do them on the way back as well.

The marshals along the course were excellent, but best not tell me how far I've gone when I am in that state, as I then work out how far it means I still have to go! But they were in plentiful supply, as were the supporters from my running club, York Postal Harriers. Their support and encouragement out on the course meant a lot and kept me going at some awkward moments.

It was a horrible experience, and I really felt I had let myself down, more mentally than physically, as I blamed the wind for the injuries!

As bad as it was, I was over the moon with my time 2:43:23. I beat the cut-off time despite being injured and running into a gusting headwind. Wow! What could I have achieved without that?

So I picked myself up, liberally applied ice spray and dosed up on ibuprofen and was now looking towards the next race.

I was hopeful that Brass Monkey was as bad as a race can get, and hoped that future races would be more like Dalby where I really started to enjoy the race. We'd see. I didn't want to tempt fate after all.

After the race we found out from the local paper that the headwind had been 50 mph that day, and I certainly felt like less of a wimp once I heard that.

LESSON: No matter how well you have trained it can still all go wrong on race day. If you're not well, don't do it.

RESULT: Distance - Half Marathon Time - 2:43:23

Sport Relief Mile - well more like 3 miles actually! April 2012

Having refused to take part in Race for Life for the past few years due to the exorbitant entry fee, all of which goes to admin and not the charity, I was pleased to find a run I could enter with my then nine year old. I should point out, perhaps, that my nine year old was not into running, and gave me a very odd look whenever I suggested she join me on a run.

I also have a friend who had asked for help getting her daughter through a three mile run she had to do in order to get her next kick boxing belt. It seemed a good idea to combine it all, with the obvious exception that I was still having physio for my buggered hip.

I was pleasantly surprised to find we could enter as a 'family' (two adults and two children) for just £15.00. How nice to see a charity event that we could afford to enter for a change. I'm not sure if any of that went to charity or covered admin but it's a hell of a lot more acceptable than the Race for Life fees are for the same distance.

We seemed to have had a lack of suitable training runs, but managed a few round the village, so I had introduced the gang to our local parkrun experience. I wanted them to understand what 3 miles would feel like on race day.

It could have gone better: my daughter sprained her ankle and managed just a third of the distance, but the rest of us finished, and I was so proud of Gail, my running buddy, as this was the furthest she had ever run. I was also pretty surprised to have made the distance myself with the hip. It was a good six minutes slower than my previous parkrun in the January but a time I was very happy with in the circumstances.

Race day dawned cloud free, and we weren't prepared for the glorious weather, but then again, who expected a mini heat wave in March!

Ours was the third race of the day and it was great to see everyone from toddlers to grandparents taking part, some in rather hot costumes it has to be said, and there was an excellent atmosphere.

We got separated just after the start so in both cases it was Mum and Daughter running together, although the twists and turns in the route meant we got to wave at each other on several occasions.

My daughter had one small stage where she asked to walk, but once she realised it hurt Mum more to walk than run she didn't ask again and kept pace with me all the way round, offering her own words of encouragement. I think I spent most of the three miles telling her how proud I was of her, whilst secretly being amazed at the stamina she was showing!

I'm not sure she was over-keen on my mini sprint finish but we crossed the line holding hands and I had never been more proud of my daughter. We stayed at the finish to encourage Gail and her daughter over the line, and I was so proud of them as well.

It was an excellent event, everyone had a great time, enjoyed the route and especially the sun and I think I may have created a monster as Gail was now looking into 10k races she could enter later in the year!

LESSON: Try and find some family races you can enter, it's a great experience.

RESULT: Absolutely no idea, this was very informal but a great deal of fun and that's why we entered it.

Where you run can affect how you run - August 2012

I'd had a very quiet year to date, still plodding along with my running, just nowhere near the level I used to be at.

My hip had been a constant problem since the Brass Monkey in January, and meant that running or even walking a mile or so led to a rather painful evening and following few days. The physio had advised that I wouldn't actually cause any more damage but it would probably hurt if I carried on running.

What's a girl to do? Quit? It's not in my nature, but, after a few months of being sidelined on the sofa I got a rather nasty shock when I tried running again. I struggled like mad with it. From running over nine miles at a time in December, I'd struggled to achieve two miles the past few months, but finally made it to three miles earlier in the month. I wanted to get back up to a 10k distance hopefully in time for the Dalby Dash in November but had to withdraw from all three of my planned Jane Tomlinson 10k runs earlier in the year.

What I had noticed was how much difference where I chose to run made, even down to which direction I set off from. I'd found a couple of routes around the village that end with a woody area, so the most scenic part of my run comes last. It's probably a similar distance to running down the main road to the ring road and back again, but it's far more attractive and pleasant as a route.

I am so fortunate that less than five minutes' walk from my house I have access to the riverside or the Common. I can avoid most of the traffic and find my circular route much easier than a down and back on the same road. I hate knowing I have to run back the same part of road.

LESSON: Experiment with different routes, sometimes just doing a route in reverse can make a huge difference to your enjoyment of the run.

OMG! I'm in London Marathon! - September 2012

I had forgotten all about entering the London Marathon earlier in the year, and wasn't really expecting to hear anything until October at the earliest. I'd not run for the last two months, partly due to injury (which wasn't going to get better but also wouldn't get any worse) but primarily due to a great deal of apathy!

The stream of tweets and Facebook updates had started early that morning from my serious running friends who hadn't got places. I flippantly joked that this was probably the year I'd get a place after several years of rejections.

So why did I enter it? Well it's far better to say you didn't get a place in the ballot, isn't it, rather than not entering at all, but also because it's something I'd actually wanted to do for a long time.

So, after the initial swearing and wanting to throw up, I rang my sister-in-law who is a veteran of many marathons including London and New York, knowing she'd have some good advice, which she did - 'Get your trainers on and go for a run!'. So that's exactly what I did.

Now bearing in mind I hadn't run in two months, I managed 3.25 miles in 38 minutes which I was bloody delighted with! You may have seen on the news about the flooding in York, but here in Strensall we seemed to be pretty free of it, other than three patches on my route through the woods which were flooded deeply beyond the width of the track - so what! It didn't stop me and I finished the run with rather wet trainers.

I was really pleased as although I could feel I was tiring towards the end of the run, I never once thought I couldn't do it.

The support from my friends, runners and non runners alike was amazing, not one of them doubted that I could do it, and it made a huge difference. One of them asked me why? It's something I'd always wanted to do, but I also think it's something I thought I could never achieve.

Getting a place meant a great deal to me, I would do my damndest to be worthy of it, and I would put the effort and training in that it required. At this distance you can't just turn up and bluff your way through it after all. I didn't know if I would finish it, but I knew that I have a stubborn streak that has seen me to the end of races before. It would take as long as it took. This race wasn't about time, it was about enjoying the whole experience, taking part and at some point, ideally sooner rather than later, crossing that finish line.

LESSON: If you enter a race ballot and get a place you can always turn it down, but if you don't enter the ballot you may never have that choice.

Some Days... October 2012

Some days, you just don't want to get out of bed, never mind run. This was one of those days. I'd not slept well all week and I couldn't get rid of a niggling cold either. The forecast for the afternoon was heavy rain which wasn't exactly motivating. All in all perfect conditions for a run - not!

I was at my client's that day, and was hoping I could fit my run in between that and the school pick up; it was that or run after tea, in the dark, in the muddy woods. I don't know about you but once I've sat down and had my tea very little tends to motivate me to leave the sofa unless it's a hot bath or chocolate in the fridge, and even then I'll try and persuade the child to go get me the chocolate.

So there you have it, incredibly tight window but I flew in the door, threw off my clothes, donned my running kit, and was out again in a flash. Bugger... before I reached the end of the street I knew this was going to be a tough run. Between lack of sleep, lack of a proper lunch and sod all energy it wasn't easy.

I was reading 'The Non Runners Marathon Guide' at that time. I actually bought it back in 2008 and it had sat on my bookshelf ever since. I went and found it the previous week when I realised I might actually have to read up on this marathon lark. Anyway, this book is as much about your mental state when running as it is about the actual running. One of the mantras it wants you to use is 'but it doesn't matter'. I'd said it over and over all week, every time I caught myself being negative I would utter this mantra. It didn't stop it hurting or help you get your breath back, but it did actually seem to help.

There's also the fact that I am an extremely stubborn bugger of course.

My running app had yet to tell me I had covered the first mile so I was coming up with all sorts of 'it doesn't matter' reasons. It doesn't matter because I am out running. It doesn't matter because I can do this. It doesn't matter because I am a stubborn cow.

I knew I could do this particular route, it wouldn't kill me, and I should have time to do it and still get to school (yes I planned on cheating and taking the car to school!), the only question in my mind at that point was would I have time to grab a quick shower. I have little points on my route that I kind of use as place markers: when I get to the second railway crossing I know I am about to hit the part of my route I enjoy (yes, the first mile and a half I am bored by), when I get out of the woods I know I am on the home straight, and when I see the pub I know I am almost home. I could cheat and cut off running the long way back down the street but then I'm only cheating myself so I don't.

Needless to say I nailed it, like I knew I would, and yes I felt lousy afterwards, out of breath, hot and sweaty, but you know what, it didn't matter. It didn't matter because right then I knew I was unfit, but I also knew that I could fix that. Just keep running and it would change.

Running home earlier that week a sound clip came on the iTunes playlist, one of my favourite quotes from Run Fat Boy Run. It's the one where Dennis says 'I'm not fat, I'm just unfit!' and you know what? Right then I suddenly realised that I was no longer fat, I was just unfit, and that was one of the best feelings ever.

I was hoping that my new 'but it doesn't matter' mantra would work for me that coming Sunday morning when I had rashly agreed to meet my friend Michelle for a joint run at 6am. Yes, 6am, a time that doesn't normally exist on any sane person's Sunday. But it was the only time we could both fit it in and it would be nice to have company on my run.

LESSON: Try and have a mantra to get you through the hard times, failing that have a cracking playlist that motivates you and makes you want to sing out loud and dance. It helps.

I'm still here and so is the lurgy - October 2012

It had been several weeks and I hadn't been able to run thanks to the lurgy. I'd almost convinced myself I'd be fit to run the following week but I was trying to find the balance between common sense and being lazy.

I can't believe how two runs just two days apart could be so different from each other. My run on the Sunday morning with my friend round the village was one of the best runs I'd had in ages, even if it was 6am on a Sunday morning. I'd forgotten that that time existed on a Sunday, and it was a little darker than I'd expected. Luckily the iPhone had a built in torch for when we hit the woods! It was one of those runs where when we finished I felt I could have gone further.

In contrast, that last Tuesday morning was nothing but hard work, coughing and spluttering the whole way round. Enjoyment didn't feature in the run at all, although the lovely hot shower at the end of it was very much appreciated.

It pretty much went downhill from there to the point that I even had time off work which, for those who know me, is unusual.

I was starting to feel more like me but suspected I had another week or so before I regained enough strength to think about running. Part of me kept thinking what a lazy bugger I was, and the other part of me was saying it was common sense to take care of me or the lurgy would last longer, and the last thing I needed to do was anything that would jeopardise my place in London next year.

I'd spoken to Martin House Children's Hospice, and although I already had my own ballot place, I'd agreed to run London to raise funds for them as part of their team. This made it even more important that I stay fit and well as they were now depending on me to help raise those much needed funds for them.

I was looking forward to a time when I could just run, without being injured, without being ill, but suspected that with my history of ME it was always going to be a problem. That said, it's something I knew I could handle. I was looking forward to getting back out there and investigating some new routes for my long runs the following year.

LESSON: Learn when to give into illness.

Gunpowder Plod 5K York November 2012

The previous lunchtime I had almost given up my place for this inaugural 5k race. I'd had a virus for several weeks and not been running and every time I went out in the cold I would start coughing. I sat back and thought about it quite a lot and decided that it wasn't on my chest, it was only 5k and there would be fireworks so I may as well give it a shot. After all, 5k seemed to be my comfort zone mileage those days round the village so it couldn't do any harm to give it a go.

What I failed to take into account was the location. The Knavesmire at York. With the exception of Brass Monkey and parkrun, every run I have ever done at the Knavesmire has been a disappointment. For a start I am not a fan of any circuit that involves you repeating an area you've already run and despite the size of the Knavesmire this often ends up happening. Couple that with appalling York traffic and you have a recipe for something that isn't going to go on the list of best things you ever did.

Quite what possessed me to enter a race on the Knavesmire on a school night passes me by right now. It must have been the promise of the firework display at the end.

For a start it was the most expensive 5k I have ever entered at £20 (and that was supposedly early bird pricing) and then had to pay extra for my husband and daughter to go watch the fireworks and the run as well. So what did I get for my £20?

- A technical t-shirt saying Gunpowder Plod worth £20 yet being sold to everyone who wasn't running for a mere £5 from the Rat Race shop tent
- A sparkler - but nothing to light it with
- A medal - not a bad medal but I did have to queue for 20 minutes to get it after finishing
- A Snickers
- A bottle of water
- A parking pass worth £10 (we were actually directed to park on the street!)
- My photo taken with Guy Fawkes (no idea how that was supposed to work but it certainly never happened, he was probably off having another sneaky fag somewhere and trying to keep warm)

The race started 50 minutes late due to late arrivals.

They were quoting a figure of 1500 runners. We all had to register on the night (for £20 I do think they could have posted my race number in advance) in the dark. The tent had no lighting in it, and it was so dark you could barely read the instructions, apparently you had to sign a disclaimer (too dark for me to read what I was signing), find your race number on a board in the dark and then go in a dark tent to be given your race number, chip and t-shirt.

Wading through the bog that was the Knavesmire I managed to find my favourite local coffee van, Poppy Coffee, and had what was to be my only hot drink of the night. With a sold out attendance of 10,000 there were barely enough catering facilities to cope. I heard tell of queues an hour long to get food at one point.

The free kids' castle and trampoline bungee were in the boggiest corner of the field. I nearly had my trainer sucked off my foot at one point as it was too dark to see quite how boggy the field was in places. Again, the sheer volume of people attending meant long queues for these as well.

The front of the stage area where the race briefing was to take place was thankfully slightly less boggy but with a start delayed by 50 minutes it was getting cold despite the THREE warm ups they asked us to do as yet another delay was announced. Of course most of this 50 minutes consisted of me coughing like a 20 a day smoker and a constantly streaming nose! I suspect I was giving Rudolph a good run for his money by this point.

Finally the race was due to start so there we were, 1500 runners being led across the Knavesmire over a little bridge in the dark and as far away from our family and friends as you could get. I suspect we were stood at the start for at least 15 minutes waiting for the line of runners to finally cross the Knavesmire to the start point. With no streaming many of the fast runners ended up at the back of the field and as we only had a narrow concrete path to run on this made for some pretty unpleasant running. The race started more with a whimper than a bang, it was only the fact the people in front started moving forward that convinced me the race was under way.

My head torch was worse than useless so I quickly decided it would be better off in my pocket and tried to stay close to runners who had the proper equipment.

I set off at a comfortable pace for me but frequently found my way blocked either by someone slower, someone walking or being cut off by a faster runner trying to find a gap to move into in front of me. As they'd warned the course was mostly unlit, no warning of where the path stopped being path and became muddy bog until the runner in front of you veered too far off and fell over as a result.

The first time through the finish was awkward as we were being told to keep to the left in a finish that was already narrowing the path and I was lucky to avoid a twisted ankle at this stage.

The promised pyrotechnics around the course were a few flashes as we set off and the odd fire thing at various markers with some canned haunted house music at one marker that didn't seem to fit.

The whole time we were on the course there was an amazing fireworks display going off in the background but it wasn't ours, it was somewhere over the rest of York.

Finally the finish post loomed in the darkness with a small number of fire torches either side of it to guide you in. I bloody sprinted that finish and I was so chuffed with myself, not only because I'd done the run, but at the speed of my finish.

The euphoria was short lived. The finish was a bit wishy washy if I'm honest, with someone shouting at you to take your chips off your shoes and drop them in a bucket. We then had to cross the bridge back over the racecourse and queue for 20 minutes to get through the tent where we received our medal and Snickers, to finally get through to try and find our friends and family somewhere on the other side in the crowd of 10,000.

When I finally got to my family I was disappointed to find they hadn't even known when the race started nor been able to see us running. That could be something to do with the entire race being in a field at the side of everything else that was going on and being in the dark.

By this point I'd started to really feel the cold, but at least I'd warmed up whilst running. Yet, there were still no fireworks. After yet another announcement of a delay the crowd actually started booing! Who can blame them? It was a freezing cold night in a boggy field, there were lots of children present, it was a school night and the fireworks were over an hour late starting. I'd like to say the fireworks made up for it all. They were okay but they weren't wow, and frankly after being in a cold muddy field for four hours I needed wow!

The bonfire had been lit at 6pm but was so small it probably burned out before most people managed to get to the Knavesmire and certainly couldn't be seen whilst we were running.

So I had no idea how long it took as despite timing chips there was no clock at the finish, and as no one knew what time we actually finally started they weren't able to guess my time.

Would I do it again? No. All the buzz and euphoria of getting back out there and running again, and feeling like I'd run well, was ruined by everything around the race, not least the farce that was trying to get home after the event. Next time someone asks me if I'd like to go for a run that involves the Knavesmire I think I'll run in the opposite direction, and as for fireworks, I'll go to the pub in the Village. I'm sure we'll enjoy the whole experience a lot more and spend a lot less in the process.

It was a valiant first effort by the organisers, Rat Race, but so much went wrong that it spoiled my evening.

LESSON: If you're going to run at night invest in a proper headtorch, not the less than a tenner ones you buy from discount stores.

RESULT: Distance - 5k Time - 36:54

Bring it on! - December 2012

I don't know about you but a New Year to me feels a lot like a clean slate, a fresh start, and most of all, an opportunity to put any negativity from the previous year behind me.

I sat down and worked out my training plan for London. Did you know that come January it would only be 16 weeks to London? And 16 weeks seemed to be the same length as most of the training plans I'd been considering.

I'd been reading 'The Non-Runner's Marathon Trainer' by David A Whitsett. It's aimed at complete novices so was perfect for me. The most important thing I'd gleaned from it was not to have a time target.

When you're running it's important to have the correct kit, to be properly fitted for your running shoes, but the most important thing of all is your mindset. If I set myself a time target and didn't achieve it I would have failed. If the only goal I had was to finish that was a heck of a lot more achievable.

In the end I'd decided to follow the Runners World 'Get You Round' training plan. With four runs a week, instead of focussing on mileage it was asking me to run/walk for a set amount of time instead.

I was a bit put off by a run/walk approach initially, but then we are talking about a marathon, and they do say their 'Get You Round' pacing team normally pass around 3000 runners on the way round the course. With a goal of just finishing this would be ideal for me.

The training even fitted in with my running club night, and as it was set to start on 1st Jan seemed meant to be.

However, as you may recall, I'd been ill or injured for most of 2012 and I'd be lying if I said the thought of what was to come didn't scare me silly. December had been a horrendous month for me health-wise, and even though by the end of the month I was feeling better than I had, I was still feeling lousy.

But then again I just needed to look at a few of the people around me. I have a friend who has a heart condition but ran a marathon, another who has cancer and is running 100 marathons and a friend with pretty serious epilepsy who ran 9 marathons in one year alone. If they can do that was I really going to let ME beat me?

I have a great network of supportive running buddies who I knew would help me through the next few months, either mentally or by joining in and supporting me by running with me. I had friends who would advise me on the nutrition side (as long as they found some way to include chocolate in the plan that is!) and who would help me with a good old verbal kick up the butt when needed as well.

So really I had nothing to worry about did I?

LESSON: Look at several training plans and find the one that not only gives you the result you want but fits in with your lifestyle as well.

We're off - London Marathon training has started - Jan 1st 2013

After weeks of being ill, months of not running and let's face it, several sleepless nights worrying about it, the training plan for London had started. It seems appropriate that it fell on the first day of a shiny new year.

Even the weather was helpful; the persistent rain had finally cleared, leaving a beautiful blue sky, albeit a slightly deceptive one because, it was a lot colder than it looked!

I'd received some new Under Armour running kit so aside from my head and fingers I didn't feel the cold, and I suspect the really painful headache on one side of my head above my ear was more cold than headache. I would make sure to wear my running hat next time!

The plan merely asked for 20 minutes of run 3 minutes and walk 1 minute on this first run. Foolishly I wondered if I'd be able to do run/walk or if my legs would just want to run, my normal route being a little over 3 miles round the village. I needn't have worried. My body seemed to have forgotten everything it knew about running so the walk breaks were needed.

The biggest obstacle was the phlegm - my chest was clear but my nose was like a dripping tap, which, coupled with running, left me choking and spitting - I hate spitting with a vengeance but didn't have much choice.

I'm used to running to a distance so guessed my route wrong, I managed 2 miles in around 23 minutes and walked the rest of the way home.

I also didn't programme the intervals into my running app correctly, I thought they'd automatically repeat and when they stopped I found I had to concentrate on my watch instead which wasn't ideal. At least I knew what to do now in advance of the following days' 30 minute run/walk.

I would either have to run with my 10 year old the following day or run in the dark on my own in the evening. I'd originally been concerned she wouldn't keep up but now, after that performance, suspected it might well be the other way around!

This first run was a lot harder than I expected, but it was done, it didn't kill me, and I learned some good lessons from it to carry forward.

At this point I honestly couldn't see me crossing that marathon line in just 16 weeks, but, you never know, I seem to remember thinking I'd never manage a half marathon last January and I did it.

The hardest part was over - getting started. From now on it would be a downhill countdown to London, and I was sure that as every mile was run, my confidence and belief would return.

LESSON: If you're using a running app programme it the night before and double check you did it right.

What a difference a day makes - 2 Jan 2013

So day two of the marathon training and it couldn't have gone any differently to the previous day if I'd tried!

The plan called for an extra 10 minutes, but the walk time was increased to two minute intervals.

It was also raining and I had to take my 10 year old daughter with me as she was still on school holidays.

I wasn't holding out much hope.

The biggest problem the previous day had been the continuous drip of my nose which had caused a lot of coughing/choking. This time I had spotted the hay fever tablets in the medicine drawer next to the painkillers and thought it was worth a shot.

I could find every piece of running kit with the exception of my hat so I settled for the Nike headband thing that covered my ears, hoping that would cut out the headache.

My daughter seemed okay with the thought of run/walk but I wasn't overly optimistic. She often gets a stitch when running and wants to walk long before we're in sight of home.

The rain got heavier as we went along but we seemed to be laughing and joking for most of it, and I was really proud of my daughter; she put in a real effort for me, and it made a huge difference. I came home having enjoyed my run, unlike the previous day.

The hay fever tablet and headband seemed to work, and I managed to programme the intervals into my running app correctly as well, so it turned out to be a very positive second training run.

LESSON: Never assume in advance how a run will go, you may well be surprised.

The best thing about running is... Jan 4 2013

... the shower! Well it is for me. I love my shower. It also signals that the run is over, the stretches are done, and it's like a clean slate for the rest of the day. It's even nicer if you've been running in the rain or the biting cold.

So this was the day of training run 3 for the London Marathon. I'll be honest, I wasn't over-enthused, I'd felt pretty rough the previous afternoon/evening thanks to the post viral fatigue and coughing, so didn't feel I had woken up with the right mindset.

Quick weigh-in on the Wii Fit, showed that luckily I'd only gained a pound that week, not bad considering the junk I'd eaten and drunk. I had to try and get on track as I knew that running a marathon would be about my overall health not just running.

The hay fever tablet didn't work as well this time but at least it wasn't as bad as my first run of the year. The plan called for 40 minutes of run 3/walk 1. I'd programmed the running app the night before with the rest of the training plan, the interval facility was excellent and I loved the verbal feedback, unless it was telling me I was running too slow!

Running this marathon would not be about time, it would be about finishing, and I certainly didn't need any extra pressure.

I found this run harder but realised that when I was running, I was running too fast, and so I tried to slow it down in the last half of the route. The woods were flooded so I had to run on the road around them which was a shame as part of the pleasure of running is getting the right route.

I did it though, and having done my stretches and had my shower, I sat snuggled up in my big red fluffy dressing gown with that lovely warm glow you get from knowing you did it, you achieved today's goal.

I was still dubious about that coming Sundays' run, it was 1hr 20 of 3 min run/1 min walk, but I could do it if I took it steady, It would be good to have company on it, I'd have to see if anyone was free. I'd already got friends lined up to run with me the Sunday after.

LESSON: Have a backup plan for your route in case you have to find an alternative mid run.

Week 1 Completed - 6 Jan 2013

I sat there that Sunday afternoon having survived my first week of London Marathon training! I can honestly say that just a week earlier I hadn't thought I'd be able to do it, so was over the moon to be proved wrong.

I hadn't slept well the night before knowing that this was an 80 minute run. Friday's 40 minute run was the longest I'd managed in almost a year with the exception of that fateful half marathon last January.

I had a running buddy this time and I think if I'm honest we both expected to have to cut it short, so were both over the moon with how it went.

The key was most definitely pace, and the new run/walk plan worked really well.

I decided that for simplicity we'd just do two laps of the village, the same route I'd done on the Friday. Because we had the pace right we both felt totally fresh at the end of the first lap and were happy to crack on with lap two.

This was also the first outing for my new running belt as well as a new running app on the phone.

The new belt sat on my lower back and had a water bottle and two very generous pockets; it was recommended over on the first marathon thread on the Fetch Everyone forum and I found it comfortable and practical.

I'd been invited by a friend to try a new running app on my iPhone and as it also handled intervals thought I'd give that a go as well. I was very happy with it. It didn't tell me off for going too slow and it looked like I'd be sticking with that for the rest of the training plan.

So that first week I'd completed four runs, burned off 1,826 calories, spent 3hrs 2 mins 37 seconds running and covered 14.1 miles in an average pace of 12:55, and as a result now had a huge, smug, self-satisfied grin on my face.

The time on my feet would increase the following week but I was now looking forward to it, rather than being so daunted by it. Sports massage was due to start again the following Thursday and I was trying to eat more healthily, but I was still virus ridden and so found it too easy to give in to temptation.

LESSON: My running apps on my phone have been a godsend, not only do they keep me on track they are a great record of my progress.

Ay up - there's a Yorkshire Marathon - Jan 9 2013

If I had a pound for everyone who mentioned this to me on launch day I'd have been...well not rich, but certainly well enough off to order a takeaway that night!

No, I didn't enter, and had no intention of entering. I hadn't survived London yet, and if I'm honest, I was still not sure if I'd cross the finish running or crawling on my hands and knees. (Volunteers with spatulas and mopeds were welcomed, and if you don't know what I'm talking about watch Run Fat Boy Run, one of my favourite films).

I'd now completed six training runs, which sounded good until I worked out there were around 63 training runs in total followed by the marathon itself.

The previous training run had been okay, pretty fast for me, possibly too fast to be honest, and I did try and slow down on my next run, but I was tired when I woke up and I ran after lunch, not a good combination for me, but I did it and that's all I needed at that moment.

It still felt wrong to be seen walking, even the postman asked why I wasn't running at one point, but the plan called for run/walk intervals and I was sticking to the plan.

The Yorkshire marathon would be in October. It wouldn't go near the racecourse, starting and finishing at the University, so that was in its favour. It would go into town, past the Minster, then back out through the villages before coming back to the

University. It was being described as a fast flat course but I seemed to recall a hill at the University that my friend often threatened me with for hill training sessions. It was very expensive at £40 to enter which was quite a bit more than London but less than the Great North half marathon I guess.

I decided to reserve judgement till much later in the day as I certainly didn't need any more pressure adding to the mix right then, and in the end it filled up so quickly the decision was taken away from me anyway.

LESSON: If you're struggling and having to run at a time that' doesn't suit your training plan why not see if you can swap things around, I did and it made a huge difference.

100 Days and it's all over - 11 Jan 2013

What can I say, after a lousy night's sleep the previous evening, I wasn't the happiest of bunnies that morning. My leg was sore as heck after the sports massage the night before, I'd gained 2lb because I'd eaten so much junk that past week (totally self inflicted) so the prospect of a 50 minute run had me wanting to hide under the duvet all day.

Still, that attitude wouldn't get me round London now would it?

I'd double checked the diary and it was the next week's run I'd been looking at, duh! Only 45 minutes this time. Funny how mentally those 5 minutes made such a big difference. So I did the school run (yes I took the car, did you not read the bit where I'm knackered?) and came home ready to run.

It was colder than earlier in the week so I'd put my wind-proof jacket on, loaded up the running belt and off I went. Grey, damp, miserable day and the woods were still flooded so most of them were still out of bounds.

Looks like I managed to slow it down this time, thankfully, and the intervals seemed to be pretty constant, giving me an average 12:25 pace overall. I was happy with that.

One of the things with my running app is that when I switch it on it loves to tell me how many days are left till London - 99 to go, which means that in just 100 days this would all be over and I could happily go back to being a lazy bugger again.

However, I was wondering how the hell my body was going to be London fit in just 99 days! That sounds like nothing doesn't it? Mind you if you'd told me two weeks earlier that I would have already run 24 miles by this point in the month, I'd have laughed, so I guess as long as I stuck with the plan anything was possible.

I really needed to work on my diet, I was tired so I would eat junk, because I ate junk, I was tired. It was a vicious circle I knew I needed to break; I'd done it before and I could do it again, it was just a matter of getting my head back in the right place that's all.

LESSON: Have a countdown calendar to your next event, it helps to keep you motivated.

Snow reason to quit - 15 Jan 2013

It snowed. I wasn't surprised, it had been forecast and threatened for a while. It followed sleet on the Saturday that had left the paths on Sunday slightly icy.

We still managed our long run of 1hr 50 minutes, breaking the seven mile mark, and it felt good. Two laps of a slightly extended route round the village. Not bad for the girl who can't stand laps!

Thanks to the snow being almost non-existent on pavements, but doing an impression of sheet ice, I had donned my trail shoes. They're heavier to run in but have better grip.

Husband and child weren't enamoured of me sticking to the plan and running. I knew it was concern about my welfare on their part but I'd been running for the last four and a bit years on and off and knew my limitations.

We walked to school, me in my lovely Under Armour running kit. I say walked but there was the odd slip crossing a road, the crunch of ice under foot, and as much as possible of it walking on grass verges. Our street sadly doesn't have any and that was challenging. I'm still glad we walked rather than taking the car though.

This was to be a 40 minute session on a 3/1 interval. Starting from school meant I had to re-think the route slightly, and then again to allow for the bad icy conditions.

With a little bit of adaptation I did it. Occasionally I had to walk a really icy bit in the middle of what should have been run, but tried to make it up where it was safe to do so.

I juggled running on the path, the grass verge, the road and the best bit - the woods. I decided that on the next day's longer run I'd find a way to do the woods twice as they were safer to run in at that time and a heck of a lot prettier in the snow. Much nicer than running up and down the same stretch of grass verge a few times to make my time up!

It had started to snow gently while I was in the woods and it was lovely.

One of the parents walking home from school mentioned he was going home to his treadmill. Yes I could have found a gym and treadmill, I could have run further and faster in my 40 minutes that way, but I wouldn't have gained as much pleasure and satisfaction from it as I did from that morning's run.

I used common sense, made allowances for the conditions and thoroughly enjoyed my run that day.

With 95 days to London, I was hoping I could say that for most of my training runs!

LESSON: Have a contingency plan for your training. I didn't have one for the bad weather and continued to run in it, with the result that I got injured.

To pause or not to pause - Jan 19 2013

I was rather cheesed off with my running app this particular morning! It had let me down. It's not so much that it let me down as where it did it though.

When I was trying to increase my running time on this 'Get me round' training plan it meant that I needed to be more creative about my routes. I had to add extra streets here and there to increase the time I was actually out running.

I don't know about you but there are streets that I just don't like. The mere thought of them has me making yuk noises. It's just a street, I know, but it's there in my head that I don't like it, and I try to avoid adding it to my run route if possible.

One such street is the one to the left of the school, a long, long horseshoe. For some reason it's easier to run it left to right I've found.

So that morning I bit the bullet and included it, running right to left as well!

I was three quarters of the way round and realised that surely by now I should have had a walk interval when I checked my phone. It had paused itself and cost me five minutes. It may not sound much but when I'm supposed to run for 50 minutes I didn't want my app to show 45. I especially wanted the app to have recorded the hated street on the route.

I don't use auto pause as in the past on running apps I've found it activated when it shouldn't. All I can think of is that somehow I'd caught the screen putting the phone back in the waist pack.

Arghhh!

So despite the app showing 48:18 I did 52:31 and I'd run the street I dislike. You know what? With the exception of the sheet ice alley to get back to the school road, it wasn't that bad!

LESSON: Lock your phone before you put it back in your bag!

One Month Down - 1 Feb 2013

Safe to say that by this point I'd started having nightmares as the reality of getting a place in the London Marathon started to hit home. Come on, as many running friends as I have who've already run marathons, I'm pretty sure the majority of my friends were falling into the 'Why?' camp

I'd surprised myself by managing the whole of the first month's training, I'd clocked a respectable 80 miles (I only ran 95 miles in the whole of the previous year to put that in context), and so far, fingers crossed, it hadn't broken me yet.

I was running four times a week, up to 55 minutes at a time at that point during the week, and my longest run so far on a Sunday had been 2 hours. Some days I would go out and wonder when I started running if I could achieve that day's planned time, and every time I surprised myself by completing it. I was stronger than I thought, or perhaps it was just sheer bloody mindedness, I am a Yorkshire lass after all!

With 78 days to go to London, the accommodation was booked and so were the train tickets, and the fundraising page was set up. It was really happening!

Every time I started to wibble I would remind myself that the training hadn't let me down yet, but then 'the voice' kicked in, reminding me that no matter how well my regular runs would go, I have a habit of breaking myself in races. Thirsk, Sutton and Brass Monkey jumped out at me and 'the voice' started laughing.

Sod them. It was a fresh month, I had not only survived January but was pretty bloody pleased with myself with what I had achieved: 80 miles, over 17 hours of running time and I burned off over 9,800 calories to boot!

I nearly didn't start the fundraising page as I hadn't wanted to let anyone down who'd sponsored me, if I couldn't do it, but then realised that was only feeding the negativity.

I could do this, I would do this.

LESSON: Set up a sponsor page early in your training, it helps motivate you to keep going.

A different kind of tired - 5 Feb 2013

There seemed to be a certain amount of concern from people around me that I was running too much or taking too much on. Not in a nasty way, I knew it was in a caring way, and yes, I had been really ill in December thanks to the ME.

That last year had been one of the worst years I'd had health-wise in a long time. I'm pretty sure when the doctor advised finding a balance between activity and rest that he wasn't talking about marathon training!

However, I'd now started week 6 of a 16 week marathon run/walk training plan. I was being very sensible about the whole thing, following the plan, not pushing myself to do more, and trying to get my diet on a more healthy footing as well.

I think I'd finally cracked the over-eating that plagued me for most of December and January (it's a side effect - when I get so worn down I struggle to get back to my usual energy levels, the worse I feel the more junk I eat. I know I'm not hungry, I just eat because it's there), and I was trying to introduce a more sensible and balanced attitude to food. (Yes I was still getting to eat chocolate every day and yes I was eating more to cope with the amount of running I was doing).

Every time I'd gone out I'd wondered if that day would be the day that I failed, and every day I went out and succeeded. It was time to look at what I had achieved rather than what I had left to do. I was only around a third of the way through the plan.

I'd run for 2hrs and 20 minutes the previous Sunday! I'd covered over 11 1/2 miles. I'd never achieved that outside of a race before, and was well chuffed.

I'd been having regular sports massage which was making a big difference to the injured hip, In fact I'd say it was pretty much a niggle now rather than an injury. I think they misdiagnosed it last year to be honest.

I had a new running partner that weekend - my sister-in-law's Weimaraner, Roscoe. She came along as well and after threatening to drop out at the end of lap one before we'd even started, she completed the whole thing with me.

Now this run/walk is pretty amazing at allowing you to do more and go further. Everyone who tried it with me went from being a Doubting Thomas to a firm believer. We even found a new lap to add to the village route so I didn't have to go round three times.

We went out on a run again together, and it was a shame she had to go home again as I'd really enjoyed running with them both. My sister-in-law has run several marathons including London and New York so it was great to hear her experiences, and Roscoe is just gorgeous and so well behaved when he's running.

The point of this whole thing anyway was that I realised that yes, I was very tired most days, but it was a good tired, it came from healthy exercise, rather than the debilitating tired that comes from being ill with ME.

I was taking it steady, I was being sensible (yes it was icy that morning so I wore my Yaktrax), and I was keeping an eye on things.

Finishing a run is one of the best feelings you'll ever have!

LESSON: Celebrate what you've achieved rather than worry about what you still have to do.

A marathon is more than 26.2 miles - 6 Feb 2013

I've sat and watched London Marathon on the TV from the comfort of my sofa for more years than I care to remember. I've always been in awe of every single person taking part, after all 26.2 miles is a hell of an achievement. This awe was still there no matter how far I'd run.

What I'd never fully appreciated until now was that that final 26.2 miles you see them cover on the TV is the end of a journey that probably started months earlier.

A standard marathon training plan covers 16 weeks - that's four months of training for those few hours of race time. I'd got one of the easier training plans and I knew I'd cover around 350 miles before race day, I'd spend hours running and that's before I even got to the start line. It's also probably just a fraction of what the more serious contenders would be putting into their training.

A spring marathon like London also means training in the dark, cold, snow, ice, heavy rain and biting cold winds. Doesn't sound like fun does it? Trust me, it's not.

But every single person entering that race has their own reason for enduring the training; for some it's to beat a time, for others it's to remember a loved one, and for many of us it's to raise money for charity. I guess I was also doing it just to prove to myself that I could.

So next time you see someone cross a marathon finish line spare a thought for the months of training and hundreds of miles it's taken for them to get there.

And yes, I had rain, sleet and a biting cold head wind on my last hour long training run!

LESSON: A marathon isn't just 26.2 miles, it's months and months of training, hundreds of miles, and a lot of hard work.

I'm injured...11 Feb 2013

... and I was scared. I was scared that I couldn't stretch out, massage away or treat this one with ice. The actual pain didn't bother me, but the thought my London training might be buggered up bothered me hugely.

The run that caused it was only an hour and a half run, the walk interval had dropped from 2 minutes to 1. My calves were tight both on both the Friday and Saturday, despite Thursday's sports massage, lots of stretching and even using a foam roller for the first time.

The run went well, I knew I was faster than on previous runs but I was feeling good. I even managed to put on a fast burst at the end just so I could break 8 miles. I was over the moon when I finished.

By the time I'd done my stretches and had my hot bath it was obvious there was something wrong from the knee to the ankle on my right leg. It was weird, it felt like it was right down the side of my shin. When I tried to stand there was a shooting pain down my leg. For the first few steps I could hardly bear to put my weight on it, but once I'd got the motion going it eased off when walking.

I'd stretched and tried treating it with ice but no joy. Just sat down it was hurting, a constant dull ache.

LESSON: Regular sports massage during your training won't prevent injury, make sure you tell your therapist about ANY niggles you have as they may be hiding an underlying problem.

Ice Ice Baby... ice pack time - 17 Feb 2013

Having spent most of the week limping around I was convinced I'd buggered it all up. The worst thing was that the run responsible was one of the best yet.

There was a tiny spark of hope in the back of my mind that the lack of swelling, bruising or lumpy bits might mean it wasn't too bad. I can't remember a Thursday night sports massage ever taking that long to arrive normally.

Monday meant school run, a steady fifteen minute walk each way. Putting weight on my leg when I first stood was agony but once I got moving it became easier. It was still a long steady limp to school though.

Tuesday should have been my run day, and as is typical when you're injured it felt like everyone else was out running, including half the barracks!

Wednesday I cheated and took the car as I had somewhere to go, and was rewarded with a downfall of snow.

Thursday morning was slushy and icy so the Yaktrax got an unexpected outing on my boots for the school run. By now there was less pain on standing and just a pretty constant ache, but a lot less limping.

Thursday night finally arrived and most of the sports massage was concentrated on my calves.

Yep, I was right, the whole thing was down to really tight calf muscles. A bit of work on the ITB as well and I was delighted to be able to get off the massage bed with no wincing when my foot touched the floor. My daughter even commented that the limp had gone as well. Great!

Friday... Not so great, the tightness was already back and it felt like I'd gone back days in terms of recovery. Another run cancelled and another steady limp to school.

So... Sunday... Supposed to be 2hrs 40 minutes of run 4 minutes/walk 1 minute. Louise had already run seven miles before she arrived at my door but planned on thirteen.

The minute I set off it was uncomfortable. The walk element was okay but the transition from walk to run was really painful. I decided to drop the walks and just run for an hour instead. The first five miles weren't too bad, good steady pace, good conversation, but by the last mile it was starting to feel uncomfortable and time to head home.

I'd got a couple of lovely calf shaped hot/cold packs from a local shop in the freezer, a tube of Deep Heat and a foam roller. I was sorted.

After stretches, ice, rest and a hot bath it still hurt a lot! The 62 days to London sounded far too soon.

That said, I was disappointed I only managed six miles, but just a few months ago that would have been impossible, and I was unbelievably impressed with what I'd achieved so far.

I'm a Yorkshire lass full of northern grit and was sure I'd find a way to overcome this. I know I was expecting to crawl across the finish line on hands and knees but I really didn't want to have to start the race that way!

LESSON: You aren't supposed to keep an ice pack on for more than 20 minutes, any longer and you risk making it worse.

Run/Walk/Run - Feb 20 2013

Several of my friends had recently listened to a podcast on Marathon Talk that mentioned Jeff Galloway's Run-Walk-Run technique for long distance running. I was following a run/walk programme for London from Runners World and when I checked I found it was based on Jeff's run-walk-run programme.

I'm an advocate of this run-walk-run technique and had been amazed at the progress I'd made in my own running in just a few weeks. Yes, I was injured, but that wasn't the plan's fault. It was trying to run for two weeks in ice and snow and then not being able to recognise that it had caused a problem and getting it attended to in time. Hindsight is a wonderful thing says she who could only just make it up the stairs on hands and knees at that point!

I'd started the run/walk programme in January. Prior to that I hadn't run more than 5k in months, in fact let's not forget, even including a half marathon I only ran 95 miles in the whole of that year.

Within a few weeks I'd reached 11.64 miles on a long run. Friends that ran with me on some of the earlier runs found themselves running six miles when previously they'd never covered more than three. My sister-in-law, who has previously run several marathons, joined me on one long run and decided to go home and try this run/walk on her own runs.

I had been concerned that this run/walk would slow me down a lot but was surprised to see that I was running almost as fast as I had previously over the same distances. If anything I felt better when I finished the run/walk than I used to when I was just running.

There was an interesting debate over on my Facebook timeline from friends who were considering this technique. One commented that he was scared if he adopted the run/walk idea he wouldn't be able to run normally again.

After a week of rest for my injured leg, I went for a run. I was supposed to do two and a half hours with a run of four minutes followed by a walk of one minute and repeat. The first couple of transitions from walk to run were so painful that I decided to drop the walk breaks. It didn't hurt when I was running. I managed six miles.

If you'd asked me a couple of months ago if I thought I could run six miles solid I'd have laughed. But I did it. Okay, in hindsight, I shouldn't have done it as I really suffered for it afterwards, but the point is that this run-walk-run won't stop your ability to run a distance, it just makes it easier for you to go further than you used to.

I'm sure it's going to be a topic that has a lot of debate. I remember the week I ran just over seven miles. I was ecstatic until my husband pointed out I hadn't run it, I'd run/walked it so it didn't count. You know what, I don't care. I covered that seven miles of run/walk quicker than I used to be able to run it. How I did it wasn't as important to me right then as the fact that I had covered it.

LESSON: Even seasoned runners have found they enjoyed the run/walk programme and it's a great way of increasing your mileage safely.

Walk it off - 2 March 2013

What can I say, the last two weeks of February had been frustrating, they'd been painful, and if I had a swear box I'd have been bankrupt by March. What possessed me to run that six miles I'll never know. The run was fine once I dropped the run/walk but the after-effect was anything but. It took the best part of a week before I could do the stairs without crying out in pain, adopting a kind of crab like crawl to get up there. Not good when you consider I work from home and have two flights of stairs up to my office. Luckily I work on a laptop so was able to turn the sofa into an office.

It was also the best part of a week before I left the house. Good job it was half term, as there was no way could I have managed the school walk or even contemplated driving. Then, when I did leave the house I ventured only as far as the petrol station round the corner for a cookie and that was more than enough.

The weekend involved a bit of a walk round town on the Saturday and a mosey round a shop on Sunday, that was me finished off. I retired to bed yet again in pain all night. Sleep had not been my friend for that last couple of weeks and now I was nervous.

Thursday morning was my first attempt at walking to school; it was uncomfortable but at least the previous week's stabbing pain had gone. The sky was blue even if the cars were covered in frost and needed de-icing, and it was a cold walk, but for the first time in a week and a half I had hope. Maybe I could still do this.

By the time sports massage came round Thursday evening I was hopeful I'd have an answer, and get one I did! The instructor asked a lot of questions and then shoved his thumb in my leg and boy did it hurt. But I'd take that pain again any day, because he knew exactly what was wrong.

Apparently, and I didn't know this, there's a tendon that runs from your knee, down the side of your shin and all the way to your foot/ankle. It's called the peroneal and was as tight as tight could be. It felt like he'd twanged a very taut fat piano string when he shoved his thumb in my leg.

This explained everything, the uncomfortable feeling in my foot toward the end of a run, the achy ankle and the ache in my knees. This one peroneal was causing it all. Due to sheer ignorance I hadn't realised the early symptoms, nor that they were linked, and hadn't been able to get any treatment early enough.

A good session of sports massage involving a lot of thumb stabbing, elbows and the like left me rather red and convinced I'd be bruised and raw the following morning, but nevertheless I came out on a high. It wasn't over yet. There was still a slim chance I could do London, and I wasn't quitting yet. (I was hoping people would sponsor me still just for the bloody pain and suffering I'd endured and that's before I even got to the start line!)

No running for another week at least but we had agreed that I could start going for walks on my training days instead. I managed three miles the next day, and yes, as you guessed it was cold and miserable. I'm just grateful it wasn't raining for a change.

I covered my short three mile route. Tempted as I was to try for more I was also trying to be sensible. The walk to school as usual was slow, I can never seem to convince my daughter that a 20 min pace is too slow, so was delighted to then continue on and average a 14/15 min pace after that. Even the woods were dry enough to walk through. It felt like it was just meant to be, even if the sun was hidden.

I did the new stretch the sports massage guys showed me as well as my regular stretches, and whilst the leg ached most of the day it wasn't hurting as it had before the massage. The next morning it was tired and achy, but I could live with that.

So the plan for the next week was gentle walks and another massage on the Thursday, but at least I still had that light at the end of the tunnel. With less than 50 days till London I was still planning on being there.

LESSON: Don't try running with an injury until it's better. You'll only make it worse.

Do you have a 'Chipper Jen' - 8 March 2013

One of the books that had the most effect on me on my running journey is 'Non-runner's Marathon Guide for Women: Get Off Your Butt and on with Your Training' by Dawn Dais. I suppose it's because I could relate so closely to her.

Dawn somehow signs up for a marathon yet she isn't a runner. To her, exercise is lifting the remote control and pointing it at the TV, and her weight always seems to be against her.

The book is a hilarious and honest journey from making the decision to actually running her first Marathon, although she gets to do it in a much more exotic location than me. Even if you never plan on running one step this is still a humorous read.

Now when I run I can't say I am happy and chirpy, if I'm honest I swear quite often and I certainly never look glamorous or healthy. That's something else I seem to have in common with Dawn. I also seem to have Chipper friends in common with her too.

Chipper Jen is Dawn's running buddy. She's permanently excited, always looks great and practically bounces around. She reminds me a little of Tigger.

I have two running buddies who remind me of Chipper Jen, Cathy is always singing at the top of her voice, smiling away and when she sees a photographer in a race strikes the funniest poses. Louise is just a Duracell bunny, she has so much energy and spirit it tires me out just watching her.

Chipper Jen buddies are good. They push you, they encourage you, but they are also in danger of being slapped senseless when you hit a certain mileage and just want to collapse in a heap, while they retain their perfect poise and good humour.

I don't often get the chance to run with others and when I do it's a real treat. It's also encouraging me to try and become more 'chipper' about my own running.

LESSON: Try and be more chipper about your own running, it makes you much more pleasant when someone is sharing a run with you, and you actually will find you'll enjoy your run more.

One Step Forward, Two Steps Back - 11 March 2013

That Thursday night saw me in my usual position - laid out on a sports massage bed while a young man pummelled my leg with thumbs and elbows, trying to undo the damage I'd inflicted. It looked like it was working. The peroneal wasn't as bad as the previous week and he'd found a few knots showing it was healing.

So why did I overdo it that Friday!

I got cocky. Six miles walking at an average pace of just under 15 min miles. To say I pushed myself is a bit of an understatement. There was no doubt in my mind I was still doing London even if it meant walking most of it.

I may have been chuffed to bits at what I achieved that day but I paid for it all weekend as a result. The bloody leg was so painful, and now it wasn't only hurting but it was bringing my morale down to dangerously low levels as well.

I was tired of always being in pain. Some days weren't too bad but then I'd have a series of days like that weekend where it was constant and draining.

I even considered not doing London! That just wasn't acceptable. I needed to buck up my ideas and get back to my positive state of mind.

It just felt like one step forward, two steps back. I guess the snow and bitter cold wasn't helping.

I upped the sports massage to twice weekly, thinking anything was worth a try.

Okay, it was time for a virtual slap and a good talking to myself.

LESSON: Don't overdo it, take it slowly when recovering or you'll end up going backwards in your recovery.

Suck it up Girl - 14 March 2013

I was beginning to think the weather had it in for me. I would wake up, look out the window and see blue skies but as soon as I set foot out the door it was grey and miserable again! For my next run it was freezing, literally.

There's a huge difference between running in all weathers and walking. I'm definitely not a fair weather runner, I run in snow, ice (after all that's what got me in this mess), blizzards, rain storms and sunshine, although I couldn't quite remember the last warm run I had!

If my training plan called for two hours and I wasn't injured I'd be up and out the door whatever the weather threw at me, so why couldn't I be the same when it came to walking? I suspect it may be because walking has been something we'd done as family time on a weekend, be that a muddy walk on the common, a snowy walk or just a gentle stroll around the village or other pretty location. To now do this on my own didn't seem quite right. Not to mention the fact that, boy, do you feel the cold when you're walking rather than running! You have more time to focus as you don't concentrate in the same way you do when you run.

The week started off with me having a bit of a wibble and a pity party for myself. I'd since given myself a good talking to, listened to some sensible friends and tried to re-assure my husband that walking London would not kill me. I guess deep down I felt that walking London was failure, I was happy enough to follow the run/walk training plan, but needed to listen to the people who were telling me that however I completed London it would be enough.

Tuesday's additional sports massage didn't feel like it had helped much, but it had reduced the rather obvious limp I'd been sporting over the weekend and beginning of the week. I was hoping for more from my next session as that was focussed purely on the injury.

I wasn't sure I was going to go for a walk this particular Thursday morning, I'd put it off all week, and Thursday wasn't even a training day, but what the heck, I needed to do something to keep active. I knew I had probably overdone the pace the previous week so this was just about getting out there - a gentle if freezing stroll around the village. It took me just over an hour to do 3.48 miles. There wasn't the buzz I get when I run, nor was there any satisfaction in it. I guess I was really missing running.

I'd arranged to borrow an exercise bike for the next few weeks on the advice of my sports massage team. This was good, because even if we had another week of snow I'd still be able to keep active in some shape or form.

LESSON: Have a back up form of exercise if you're injured, talk to your sports therapist about the best form of alternative exercise for your particular injury.

The Kindness of Strangers - 15 March 2013

On my runs and walks round the village one thing that always helps is a quick 'hello' from the people you see out and about. This had been even more important whilst I was injured and was only able to walk round. Several times I'd slowed down and had a quick chat with someone I didn't know about what I was doing and who I was doing it for.

Always in this situation there were words of encouragement, even praise for what I was trying to do.

Throughout the training there was one special lady that I had looked forward to seeing. We'd chatted over the past few months and I knew she liked to go for a walk every day, she was often faster than me with her Nordic walking poles, and she escapes to the sun every year. She always had words of encouragement for me, more so those past few weeks while I had been injured and frustrated, and after just a few minutes chat with her (we often bumped into each other on my home street), I would arrive home filled with a new energy and belief.

We finally introduced ourselves in early March, after three months of hello's and chats. I was quite sad she was going away the following week and wouldn't be here for London, but she'd promised to keep in touch via my running blog, and I certainly didn't begrudge her the warmth and sun of her getaway.

That morning on the school run someone called out my name, she'd come to find me to give me some unexpected sponsorship money before she went away. To say I was touched is an understatement. My eyes were watering.

When you're out and about doing your everyday thing, please do just give a smile and a hello to whoever is running past. It can make a hard run easier, a tired heart lift a little, and makes the runner smile as well.

And if you happen to befriend a runner, like my new friend did with me, words honestly can't tell you how much that means.

Thank you so much to my new friend. You gave me faith, encouraged me and made me smile. I look forward to your return, and hopefully running into you rather than strolling into you .

LESSON: Always smile and say hello to people you pass when running, it makes it a much more pleasant run for you, especially when they smile back.

Tape it up - 21 March 2013

After my second sports massage that week it was time for a review of the injury. The peroneal was still very tight and running was definitely still out of the window. Their advice, if I wasn't doing London, would be total rest, but I was. The good news is that once London was out of the way I could fully rest the leg, no walking, cycling or cross training, and it would mend. Yay! I guess I was beginning to suspect that as it hadn't really responded to treatment running wasn't in my future. It had got better though, and just because I wasn't running didn't mean that it wasn't improving. It wasn't getting any worse, and some days I could walk without limping at all.

This session we tried something new, taping it up, to see if it would make a difference. I'd heard good things about taping.

They also recommended using the cross trainer rather than walking, I was sure there might be one hidden out in the garage somewhere, and I was still carrying on with the exercise bike.

They kept muttering about ice baths but there are some things I just can't bring myself to do!

LESSON: If you're injured ask your sports therapist about KT Tape, it made a huge difference to my recovery.

KT Tape

I'd known about Kinesiology Tape for a couple of years, having been told about it by one of my marathon running friends.

I just think of it as magic tape, but the Wikipedia definition of it is:

*"**Elastic therapeutic tape**, is an elastic cotton strip with an acrylic adhesive that is used for treating athletic injuries and a variety of physical disorders."*

There are a lot of different brands available and as a result a lot of different price points. It comes in a long roll, pre-cut, or even specially shaped pre-cut for specific injuries.

What it does as far as I know is to help injuries and healing.

I run with two different sets of taping.

I have a fancy pattern that I tape around my knees to support them. What I would say is that the tape gives you the support that my neoprene knee support used to give me, but doesn't get tight or uncomfortable like the knee support would after any length of time. I apply the tape and can actually immediately feel the support it gives me, but it's flexible so doesn't restrict any movement at all.

I then have a different set of taping to support my peroneal. The peroneal, I am informed by my sports massage guy, goes from the side of my knee, down the side of my calf, down my ankle and all the way under my foot. Trust me to damage something that covers so much. It also explains the slightly numb feeling in my right foot on long runs and the ache in the ankle. In hindsight these were the early indicators that I needed to get checked out, but just assumed they were an old ankle tear playing up.

When my peroneal became injured it was at the top near my knee so I tape right up to just below my knee. The tape starts on my ankle on the other side of my leg, comes under my foot, up the other side of my ankle and all the way up the side of my calf to just below my knee, before a second piece of tape runs from the other side of my ankle, around the back of my heel and down the other side of my foot to nearly my toes.

This gives me a really funky pink leg stripe you can see when I run, although the knee taping stays hidden under my capris. I'm not sure if I'll ever be brave enough to run in shorts with all that taping.

You are supposed to be able to leave KT Tape on for up to three days as long as you don't get a bath. It's supposed to stay put in the shower.

Me being me, and loving lobster hot baths at the end of the day, I can often be found taking mine off in the shower after my run, although I am told this reduces the healing effectiveness.

I have kept it on for a couple of days on occasion and it works, but as I found a brand I like and that works on Amazon for under £7 a roll, I just peel it off most days and put it on again when I next run.

If you check out YouTube there are loads of videos showing you just how to apply the tape depending on the type of support that you need. Even doing this I found I needed to double check with my sports massage guy that I was doing it right on the peroneal. It appears if I got the start point just slightly off the ankle area it would sometimes come loose and annoy me when running, not that it was any less effective, it was just annoying.

LESSON: You don't have to always buy the brand names but do check out the reviews to make sure that what you are buying works, many of the cheaper brands I looked at had very poor reviews.

Saddlesore - 28 March 2013

Well between a bad cold and the truly awful weather I hadn't even managed any walks for a couple of weeks. I hadn't been sat on my backside though. Well I was, but not quite in the sense you'd expect.

On the Sunday it should have been my four hour run, tapering down from that point on but, as it had been for the past few weeks, it was snowing, there was a freezing cold wind and I'm sorry, despite running in anything, I'm a wuss when it comes to walking.

I'd been making it up by cycling on the exercise bike my friend kindly lent me for a few weeks. I'd been cycling 12 miles most sessions but decided to up the ante a little that Sunday and cycled just over 26 miles.

It wasn't too bad, I set the exercise bike up in the kitchen, watched a movie or TV on the iPad and the Kindle sat nicely over the display on the bike so it didn't distract me from how far I still had to go.

My legs held up quite well considering, I'd taped them up using a different format that I found on the KT website and it was fine afterwards, which is more than could be said for my sitting down again.

Guess it had been a few years since I was last on a bike in any shape or form and boy did I know about it all that week and over the weekend.

I missed the next planned cycle as I was so full of cold I took a day off from everything; I'd have to catch up over the next couple of weeks.

With only three weeks to go I wasn't panicking yet.

LESSON: If you're cross training indoors see if you have space to set up a TV or iPad to distract you from the exercise, without the change of scenery you get from running outdoors it can be easy to get bored.

I'm still here! - 13 April 2013

A couple of friends had commented that I'd disappeared off the radar over the previous few weeks. It was nothing serious, I'd just had a grotty virus that laid me low. It's one of the things I suffer from with the ME; if I get a virus it takes me a while to get over it.

The weather was sunny but cold over the preceding week which meant I really didn't feel like going on long walks, although I had managed a couple. I'd also done a couple of 26 mile sessions on the exercise bike. The only trouble with the bike was that my knees started to hurt. I'd decided the bike should be left alone until after London and was hoping to get a long walk in that weekend if the weather held.

The good news was that the enforced rest from the virus meant the leg was feeling a lot better. There was no limping at all now, and the ache was now just in the ankle when I walked any distance.

The plan was still to walk most of London the following weekend, but now I was hopeful I'd be able to run the last part at the Mall.

In the meantime I was trying not to think about just how far 26 miles was in a straight line, four walks round the village is the same distance but sounded a lot more achievable.

By now I was snotty, nervous, excited and daunted but determined as well. Bring on London!

LESSON: Keep your friends updated on your progress.

I've got a Spatula - 15 April 2013

So what? You may say. I'll be honest, to most people just about to take part in their first marathon it will make no sense at all. But if you've ever watched my favourite film 'Run Fat Boy Run' you'll appreciate what a spatula means.

Not only does a spatula help Dennis get round when he damages his ankle but it's part of the training. His landlord really cares about Dennis, and, in the role of Assistant Coach, follows him on his training runs on his little moped and applies the spatula when he's not going fast enough.

The fact that someone, namely my lovely marathon running friend Kelly, thought enough of me to go get a spatula especially engraved for me, means so much. It's one of the most thoughtful things anyone has ever done for me, and yet so many people won't understand it, even the lady engraving it queried the content but it couldn't have been any better.

Kelly had some really useful advice on what to put in my kit bag for after. I've never bothered with a kit bag before so this was really useful.

I'd already planned on leggings, a warm top and comfy slip on shoes but she suggested things like a toothbrush and toothpaste, wet wipes, deodorant, clean underwear and a hairbrush. Things that would make me feel human again once I'd crossed that finish line.

Kelly took me to the pound shop to buy a pound poncho in case it was raining before the start, as the 'throwaway' cardigan I was planning on abandoning at the start if it was cold wouldn't keep me dry if it was raining.

At that point rain was forecast for the afternoon of the marathon, and with the weather we'd had so far, anything was possible!

Kelly gave me an extra roll of KT tape just in case I ran out. She's a very practical lady is our Kelly.

It was so useful to chat to someone who'd been through this. Most of the books I'd read about marathons didn't cover what I classed as the really practical stuff, the things I needed to know before I set off.

Now having sorted the things for my kit bag I was ready for it. In fact now, I just wanted to get it over with.

Aside from the physical side of training for a marathon some days can be very tough mentally, especially when you're injured, and I have to say that I had some fantastic emotional support from friends and family.

I honestly don't think one of them ever said that I couldn't do this. There may have been expressions of concern over whether I should do it, considering the injury, but not one of them ever made me feel I wasn't good enough.

I know that some were concerned that I was so determined to participate and finish that I'd do myself some long term damage. I'm stubborn, yes, but I'm not stupid. Although it was rather funny hearing my ten year old tell her Dad that Mummy would be fine and she'd cross that finish line even if it was on her hands and knees. She knows me so well!

I was surprised by how comfortable I was about the coming Sunday.

I was happy I could do the distance, and it would take as long as it took, apparently the cut off was eight hours which seemed like more than enough time for me.

I knew that at various points on the course there would be people supporting me and shouting for me, although I suspected in the midst of everything I might not actually see them, but I knew they'd be there and that was enough.

I knew what tube and what train I needed to get and when, to get where I needed to be when I needed to be. I knew where I was meeting up with my family afterwards.

I knew, that whatever happened, however it went, this was going to be one hell of an experience that I would never forget, and that WHEN (not if) I crossed that finish line I would be so bloody proud of myself and there would be so many others supporting me.

I was itching to get out there and run, but it was too close now and I daren't risk it. I simply consoled myself with the image of me running across that finish line on Sunday instead.

I took that spatula to London with me. My only regret is that it was just a little too large to go in my running bag on the day.

LESSON: Always carry tissues with you as if you're like me, people will constantly make you cry with happiness at various points during your marathon training, especially in that last week.

Wet, Windy and Wicked - 17 April 2013

It was raining when I set off on my 'run', it was bloody cold and as usual the wind was in my face, for some reason it's never at my back. But it didn't matter because this was my last training session before London, my last chance to see if I had it in me or not.

On the Monday night I'd gone for a three mile pootle round the village with my friend and her daughter, and as much as I wanted to run I didn't. I just did a fast-paced walk but it was far below my target pace of 15 min miles. The sun was out, the company was good and that jaunt did me a lot of good. I really enjoyed it.

This run wasn't as much about testing the legs (the sports massage girl seemed to think they were in pretty good shape apart from the injury), but was about making sure my head was in the right place for Sunday.

The weather that morning wasn't exactly enticing; I don't know why I find it so hard when I know I'm walking, as I have no qualms about running in bad weather, but then there were no guarantees it wouldn't rain on Sunday so I needed to get out there and get this in the bag.

From the get go I was enjoying it, the leg felt so good I was sure I could run, but I couldn't afford to bugger it up. I was saving the running for Tower Bridge and The Mall. The first mile went past in just under 15 minutes and it was good for the soul. After that I kept being surprised every time the app told me I'd completed another mile and under my target time. I wasn't focussed on the distance this time at all, I was more interested in pace and scenery.

Granted a windy, cold rainy day may not seem scenic but there were the new spring flowers, a couple of bored looking sheep, geese crossing the field and even a squirrel running across my path. Okay there were the usual cars and buses to dodge on the road as well, and the road seemed busier this time for some reason. I even took my jacket off just after the first mile and ran in my Martin House Children's Hospice vest. I was more than warm enough thanks to my gloves and the heat I was generating.

Each mile was yet another cheer, another reason to celebrate, and you should have seen the spring in my step going over the kerb at mile five. I felt like Tigger - full of bounce! A couple of weeks ago I could barely walk round the block without getting out of breath.

Don't get me wrong, my legs ached, but this time it was that good ache that comes from exercise rather than aching because of injury.

I'd started taping around my knees rather than using knee supports and it was a lot more comfortable. I just needed to get the taping right on the peroneal for Sunday, the ankle had felt a bit weak over that last mile.

The good news was I covered seven miles, and that meant I could officially say London wasn't even four times round the village! I could handle that.

I was so looking forward to it now. I had an amazing support network behind me, encouraging me, believing in me, and it had rubbed off - I believed in me too.

LESSON: I found that concentrating on my walking speed and finally getting it under 15 min miles consistently made a huge difference to my running when I was able to start again.

Virgin London Marathon 21st April 2013

I've started writing this chapter a week after the marathon and already it feels so surreal, almost as if it didn't happen.

I know I have a shiny and very heavy medal, a finisher's T-shirt and a lot of photos to say it did, but I'm still surprised when I see them.

I guess I've given away the secret; perhaps I should have kept you in suspense and made you wait until the end of the chapter to see how I did, but I'm not that cruel.

The week before the marathon can best be described as numb. I was so calm about it, aside from one huge wibble returning from school one morning. The wibble was always going to happen so there was no point getting stressed about it. It was one of my busiest weeks in a while as we also had a Spanish host student staying with us.

Getting to the Expo on the Saturday in time to register was probably my biggest worry of the whole weekend, but we made it. It was an expensive journey as we failed to see the Oyster card scanner when we switched from the tube to the DLR and got charged £14 each for that journey.

The registration was really quick and efficient. I had visions of queuing for ages but just a few minutes after entering I had my number and my tag for my shoe. We didn't spend long at the Expo as I was conscious no one had eaten yet and it was now late afternoon, so we set off for pasta, having received a text from my sister-in-law advising we eat pasta at lunchtime rather than in the evening. As she's completed several marathons I thought it wise to heed her advice, although I can't say I had much of an appetite, as my recent penchant for snacking and eating junk seemed to have abandoned me.

We didn't spend long in London, we were all tired and ready to head back to the apartment for an early night.

I'm really pleased we spent a little extra and chose an apartment over a family room in a hotel. There wasn't a great deal of difference cost-wise and the extra space was really welcome.

I booked us into Earls Court as I wanted somewhere fairly close to the finish, and the apartment was just a short walk from the tube.

I crashed out on the bed quite early leaving the rest of the guys to watch bad TV as is normal for a Saturday night while I painted my nails, put some cooling foot mask on and played around on Facebook and Twitter.

I decided to call it a night at 9pm, having laid out all my kit for the morning. On giving my phone one last check I received the most amazing message from a friend:

"It's all going to be a bit crazy in the morning for you and I don't want to interrupt. But know this: you are AMAZING and INSPIRATIONAL and a JOY to behold. I hope you cherish the day – the atmosphere, the crowds, the experience – and I can't wait to congratulate you when you pass that finish line! Love you lots! xx"

I can't tell you how heart warming that was, it was the last thing I read before I fell asleep.

I woke just after midnight and decided to check my sponsor pages, I'd hit the magic £1,000.00 mark while I was asleep. I went back to sleep a very happy bunny.

Sunday morning was bright and cheery, although hardly anyone else appeared to be awake in the houses and hotels around us.

After a quick shower I covered myself in sun cream (just in case), applied copious amounts of KT tape to both knees and my peroneal, applied Vaseline everywhere I'd been told to, and donned my running kit including the black armband I was wearing in respect for Boston Marathon.

I made sure my running bag was packed, my kit bag had everything I needed for after, and I was off.

The streets on the walk to the tube were devoid of runners but as soon as I hit the tube station it started. The platform was full, and they all looked as if they knew what they were doing!

A couple of other runners I talked to were heading to Blue Start and offered to help me find my way, despite my carefully planned out times and train numbers. Cath, the lady stood next to me, spotted my Martin House vest and told me she was running for them as well. Out of an estimated 36,000 runners and Martin House only having a team of 15, what were the odds of that happening!

We walked together to the station for the train to Blackheath and that's the first time the numbers really started to add up. The train was jammed full. The journey to Blackheath seemed to take forever, then getting off the platform took ages but I found myself stood in the car park at the station, enjoying the sun and the smell of the market set up in the car park, while I waited for Cathy, my running partner, to arrive.

Within seconds the station had emptied, the next train came in, the station emptied and so on. It worked really well.

It was great to see Cathy, we used to run together when we were training for Brass Monkey but hadn't seen each other in ages.

The plan was we'd head to the start together, cross the start and then see how long we could run together for.

Blackheath high street was an amazing sight, and I couldn't believe it when I saw someone I knew. Between bumping into a fellow Martin House runner and then my friend I was convinced it was a good omen and today was going to be a good day.

As we walked onto the start area both Cathy and I kept saying we couldn't believe we were finally here and that this was real. It was good to know we were both so in awe of the whole experience.

After posing, and I mean posing, for photos together Cathy, blagged an interview on Italian TV! We've not been able to find the coverage yet but I do remember the guy interviewing her was rather fit!

The kit bag lorries were lined up and manned by the most gorgeous little girls wearing oversized t-shirts. Of course I had to take a photo for my scrapbook, as well as several others just of the start area. This was like nothing I'd ever encountered before, but in a good way.

One of the TV images that always made me laugh when I watched was the size of the queues for the toilets. In reality there are around ten or so toilets laid out in a U shape for each queue, so it does go down quickly.

We had been given a leaflet in our pre-race goody bag at the Expo advising us they were offering female urinals this year, with instructions on how to use the cardboard funnel. Needless to say I decided not to brave that new experience on race day!

The wheelchair race start was being shown on a huge monitor, not that I was paying attention, and a huge cheer went up from the crowd. I was too busy soaking up all the sights and the experience.

Walking to the start we bumped into our fellow club runner. How, with a starting line up of 36,000 people could you bump into someone you know, then I bumped into Cath, my fellow Martin House runner, whom I'd met at Earls Court earlier that morning.

Because we were at Blue Start we didn't have the huge crush of runners that were at red. Cathy told me that Blue Start was for ballot winners, whilst red was for those with charity places.

That said I couldn't see the start line, or even hear the announcers. I'd been expecting a thirty second silence in memory of Boston Marathon, but way back at the back of pen five (for slow people like me who'd estimated 5:30 as a finish time when we entered the ballot) all we heard was a massive cheer and the crowd slowly started to move.

According to the official stats it took me 16 minutes to reach the start, although it felt much quicker. We hit the start, started the Garmin and the running app on my iPhone and we were off.

Safe to say I couldn't match Cathy's pace and we were soon saying goodbye.

Having read Alexandra Heminsley's book 'Running like a girl' I was cautious of high fiving the children lining the route but thought what the hell. Carefully watching for the kerb I spent the next few miles high fiving anyone who offered.

Right from that start line the crowds were out supporting us, and as a runner, I can't tell you how much difference they made.

There's something so special about seeing the look of joy on a small child's face when you give them a high five. It was me that felt honoured, from the start they were reading my name on my T-shirt and calling it out, telling me well done and I could do this. Even if they couldn't read my name they'd call out "come on Martin House!"

Within the first mile I felt like a fraud. Here I was walking along when I was taking part in a marathon. It felt wrong and I desperately wanted a sign saying 'I can't run, I'm injured so fast walking instead!'.

Checking the Garmin I was delighted to see that not only was I beating my 15 min mile pace I was closer to 12:30 pace. I was slightly concerned that I still had a hell of a long way to go, but it felt good so I thought I'd stick with it for a bit longer.

It was already feeling really warm and I regretted not bringing water with me, I just wasn't used to this as my training had all taken place in the ice, snow, blizzards, rain and cold.

Within a few miles I could already see casualties, people on the side of the road stretching out cramp, or looking as though they were in pain. It's at times like this you wonder what the hell you are doing!

A water station came up fairly quickly, which helped, and after a few mouthfuls I chucked the bottle in my running bag pocket and carried on.

There were some great costumes, and the crowd really got behind the people in costume, but I did feel sorry for them in the heat. It must have been very uncomfortable, I even saw one guy stripping off his sleeved running top as he was too warm.

By the time I made it to the point where we merged with the other starts my side of the road was fairly empty then, looking to your left and coming down the hill towards you is a sea of bodies, filling the whole width of the dual carriageway, and all moving faster than me. It was an inspiring sight. The sea was predominantly made up of runners wearing charity vests. Several of the vests had pictures of people they were running in memory of, and whilst that was sad, it was great to see so many people running for charity.

Where I could I was still keeping to the side of the road so I could high five the children, and so I could try and stay clear of the faster people merging in behind me.

I started to recognise parts of Greenwich, and have to say the Cutty Sark looked amazing in the sun. I was waving at a giant Penguin stood atop the bar next to the Cutty Sark when I heard a huge cheer and my name being called out. It was Alyson and the gang of supporters from Martin House. Wow, that felt really special.

Not far past this was the seven mile mark, I'd made it once round the village already and was still feeling good.

I had little milestones in my head to keep me going round the route, the next one being some friends from running club at a pub at the 11 mile mark.

Sadly around ten miles I realised I had a problem. My left foot really hurt every time I put my weight on it, the sole of the foot felt raw. I wasn't brave enough to stop to see what I had done, and reasoned that taking my shoe off would be a mistake so kept going.

At the 10 mile marker my phone told me I'd done 11 miles. As much fun as all this high fiving was, it was adding miles, the blue line to follow, signifying the shortest route on the road, always seemed to be the opposite side of the road to the crowd.

There was so much noise and activity at the pub I missed my friends and carried on.

There was a real party atmosphere amongst the supporters, people dressed in dinner suits and fancy dresses hanging out of top floor apartment balconies, families with picnics at the side of the road, or even families who'd dragged the sofa out to the side of the street to watch the proceedings, whilst on the opposite side of the road a huge family gathering was enjoying a barbecue!

All along the route people were offering drinks, jelly babies, Haribos, Mars bars and even Cornetto ice creams! I think my personal favourite were the Starburst sweets as they were most refreshing, and one kind lady even passed me a plastic glass of coke. It wasn't till somewhere around mile 20 I debated the wisdom of taking sweets from total strangers, and wondered what they might have done to them, but in all honesty I was so grateful for the generosity and kindness they were showing it would have been churlish to refuse, and they were pretty refreshing as I've said.

The next milestone was Tower Bridge, just before the half way mark, and I had planned on running the bridge. No chance now.

I snapped a photo just before we got to the bridge, and was in awe crossing over it. I missed the first photographer so that photo shows I wasn't feeling too comfortable, but spotted the next one and gave him a thumbs up!

Mile 12 was a new milestone, it was further than I'd managed to run in training.

Mile 13 took me into new territory running-wise, I'd never done more than a half marathon previously.

When I hit the big red mat I didn't realise it signified half way; I also didn't see the photographer there and as a result they are some of the worst photos from the day.

As you hit mile 13 the opposite side of the road is mile 22 and once again there's a sea of bodies filling the whole width of the road, this time running in the opposite direction, and they only had four miles to go. The crowd at this point was amazing.

At this stage I really was wondering what the hell I was doing, who was I kidding, there was no way I should even be taking part. Not only did I still have half the course to go but that half contained the really hard part of the course, Canary Wharf, where the seasoned runners said even they struggle.

But 13 miles is just one mile short of 14, and 14 miles is twice round the village! Come on girl.

Despite the pain in my foot I was still pulling under the 15 min pace I'd set myself.

All around the route there were toilets. At each one there were queues, but not in a nice line down the path, no, they queued the width of the road. Between dodging discarded water bottles that filled the width of the road, threatening to trip us up, us poor back runners also had to cross to the far side of the road and navigate the narrow gap the queuing runners had left us.

I was really pleased not to have to join these queues, until at mile 17 I realised I needed to. Suddenly there wasn't a toilet in sight! Typical. The Marshal told me they were 100 yards down on the right but I didn't see them, it was a mile down on the left before I found one. Luckily most people didn't need them at this stage so there was hardly any queue.

Having never covered 18 miles before my legs were none too keen on being asked to work in the confines of a portable loo! I felt like I was on a moving ship despite being on solid ground, and my swollen fingers (almost twice their normal size by now) even struggled with my running Capris. The closest comparison I can think of is for you to imagine you're using a portable loo when you're blind drunk. I think it's a similar feeling.

Onwards I went and the phone rang, the family were at Canary Wharf station. Had I passed the 30k marker yet? Why the heck, when I'm running a race that's 26 miles, would I be taking notice of kilometre markers! At this point I'm convinced I've already passed them and am starting to feel really sorry for myself when I spot my sister-in-law's blonde head bobbing towards me in the crowd. She tells me my daughter is just around the corner, and she'll let them know I'm on my way.

Cue tears at the thought of seeing my daughter. I know I can't let them see how much it's hurting, or how hard it's feeling right now so I plaster on a smile and head over to them.

You need to realise that for the last 18 miles I've been on my own, I've seen loads of runners greet their families, get hugs from friends and so on and right now I'm feeling lonely and hard done by. Having said I would be fine if they weren't there, I was wrong. The huge morale boost it gives you when someone you know gives you a hug, and tells you well done, is priceless. I know it's no fun for the supporters standing around for hours on end, but seriously, it means the world to the runner.

After several hugs from my daughter and a bottle of water from my husband (he didn't appreciate me pouring it over my head but it made a good photo), I was off again, re-charged and knowing I could do this, no matter how much it may hurt.

The next milestone was coming up, at mile 19 I only had to do once round the village, and I knew I could manage that!

The Garmin battery died at mile 20. I could no longer keep an eye on my pace and keep under that magic 15 min pace. I'd gone over on a couple of miles but had somehow kept under it for the most part. Whilst the phone was still working (I was using a back-up charger), I could hardly hear it for the crowds and the music en route.

Just past mile 20 I had a stabbing pain in my left heel, it felt like a stone in my shoe, I ended up taking my shoe off to check, but there was nothing in my shoe, which I managed to get back on (thank god for elastic laces) and carried on, suddenly the pain got really bad and then thankfully disappeared. We later discovered it was a huge blister on my heel that had popped.

The phone died on me just past mile 24 on the phone, which in reality was just past mile 22 on the course (I know but I couldn't help it, the high fives really helped keep me going). It's about this time the sun goes in as well, almost as though it was telling me I should have finished by now!

Mile 22, I never thought I'd get here when I was on the opposite side of the road, and I'd done it. Fetchpoint was coming up (the cheer point for the Fetch Everyone online running community), and I got another hug, and with it another breath of life.

I have no idea where I am in most of the photos that were taken from this point on unless there's an obvious landmark in them. I remember feeling like every mile was two miles, then a long dark tunnel filled with music and motivational quotes on floating white orbs. The tunnel was rather surreal to be honest.

I do remember looking down the length of the Embankment and thinking I can't possibly go that far!

Whilst my feet were really hurting now, the ankle and knees were holding up really well. There was a bit of an ache in the ankle but nothing compared to what I had been expecting.

The crowds had thinned out massively and lots of people were heading off home but the rest of the route was still lined with people, albeit one deep now rather than pavement deep.

I'd been told that having your name on your shirt helps, and it really does; what I hadn't expected is how sincere people sounded when they were calling out your name.

The Embankment was possibly the hardest part of the marathon for me, but as with the rest of the course whenever I started to doubt I thought about the people at home who believed in me, who thought I could do it, and if they believed then so could I. I honestly believe that 75% of that marathon was mental.

I finally turned the corner into Westminster, hoping to see the family again but they weren't there. I was gutted. As I passed Buckingham Palace and turned into the Mall the tears started, I'd done it. Just a few hundred yards and I'd have finished. Of course I couldn't even cry properly as I was so bloody tired, but despite how it looks in the photos, they were tears of joy and pride.

The grandstands were empty, and they were even in the process of packing up, but this was the final straight and I was going for it. As I started to run for the finish I looked to my left and there they were - my family was in one of the grandstands, cheering me on. A photographer caught the look of sheer joy on my face when I spotted them, and it will always be one of my all-time favourite photos.

I'd been concerned that I wouldn't be able to find them, my phone was dead, and as everything else was packing up maybe the reception area I'd arranged to meet them in would also be closed.

But no, they were there, they saw me cross that finish line at a run and complete what, for me, has been my best race experience to date.

You go through the finish over a little bridge so a man can cut off your tag from your shoe, a silly little thing but it really impressed me, and then they put your medal round your neck. It sounds silly and ungrateful but by this time my back and shoulders were painful and it weighed a ton, but there was no way I was taking it off!

And I'd done it. 6hrs 32mins 35 seconds.

I'd had a loose target of 6:30:00 and considering how much the last sixteen miles had hurt I was over the moon not only at finishing, but with my time.

We later discovered that the reason it hurt so much was a collection of nine blisters on my left foot, some of them extremely deep. I've never had blisters from running before, and can only think it was a combination of softened feet from the Vaseline and foot masks that week, and the heat.

It doesn't matter, the hurt is forgotten because I bloody well did it!

And, let's put it this way, Mo Farrah quit at 13 miles, now how many people can say they've been in the same race as Mo Farrah and finished it before him!

LESSON: This first marathon was the most amazing experience, but so much of it is lost in a fog. Try and write down as much as you can when you get home so you can remember it properly later on.

The Facebook Marathon

Anyone who knows me would tell you that I am a social media addict, I am normally permanently connected to either Facebook, or Twitter or both. I had originally contemplated posting updates as I went around the course knowing that I would be walking, even if it was just 'I've done once round the village', 'I've done twice round the village'. In the end that didn't happen because in the first half I'd found myself doing better than I had expected pace-wise and didn't want to mess around with a phone, and in the second half I just didn't have the energy.

Unusually for me I didn't even check Facebook and Twitter when I'd finished. In part this was due to the phone battery having died on me, but also because I was just so exhausted it could wait.

This meant that until much later that evening I was in total ignorance of the saga that had been unfolding on Facebook between my friends and family. I'd probably been back at the apartment a couple of hours before I could get up enough interest to log on.

When I start running with my running app it posts an update to my Facebook page, allowing my friends to actually follow my route and progress on a map. I use this to keep me accountable, if I quit during a run someone somewhere will see it. Virgin London Marathon also have a website where you can track a runner's progress and I had given this link to family and friends earlier in the week. Whilst I'd thought maybe the odd one would be checking occasionally during the day it came as a total shock to me to find out that several family and friends had been glued to their screens all day.

When my phone died on me around the 22 mile mark it was annoying. I did wonder for a moment if anyone would have noticed but thought no more of it. That is until my mother told me to check out my Facebook timeline when I finally managed to get to a phone and call her about half an hour after I had finished.

The comments started as soon as I crossed the start line and were mostly being proud of me and telling me I could do it. Some friends commented that they were with me every step of the way, and from the rest of the timeline it's obvious that they were, I really wish I'd known that as I was going round, although I had known they were with me in spirit.

I can see where they spotted me just before Tower Bridge, and then the comments about me making it 'twice round the village', before they get to that last 'once round the village'. By this point there's even a conversation going on between my mother and Kelly about how well I am doing, although they have never met each other.

The comments from the 22 mile mark are so amazing, as well as funny. My mother and several others couldn't refresh the page as the app had crashed and Kelly told them the Virgin Marathon page was showing I'd done 40k in 6:10:19, just 2k to go. She then had to translate that into English for my mother who, like me, prefers to deal in miles.

I later found out there had been a series of panicked phone calls between family members when the running app died, 'she wouldn't have quit, not that close to the finish' was the general consensus. They knew me too well.

Kelly kept my Facebook friends updated over that last 2k letting them know when I'd finished.

One friend told me she and her daughter had been watching and cheering at each marker all through the day and had cheered out loud and jumped up and down when I finished.

When you're out there, feeling alone, you're not. Even though I hadn't seen those comments while I was out on the course I knew deep down that they were supporting me, encouraging me, and of course Kelly was threatening use of the spatula throughout the Facebook conversation bless her!

LESSON: Try and have something in place to let your friends know how you did, and let them know how they can track your progress if that option is available.

Running because you can, not because you have to! 3 May 2013

I went on a run on my own, because I could. There was no training plan to tell me I had to, no race looming that required training, just an opportunity for me to have some 'me' time and see what I could do if I just did it.

The previous Friday had been my first run since London, and in reality my first run since I got injured. I ran just over four miles without stopping just to see if I still could. It was great to be back out there, but it was hard work.

I wanted to test myself, to see if I could still run, so I did. It felt absolutely bloody fabulous. I was back!

Since then I'd been out on a couple of 5k run/walks with a friend I am helping to run her first 10k, she's doing well and the 3/2 run/walk we're starting with seems sensible to ease me back into running after my injury. Last thing I want is to end up on the injury bench again.

This session was running just for me, because I could. No clear idea of the route, I decided most of it on the run, no pressure over pace or time, just enjoy whatever happened.

About two thirds were on the road and the last third running back down the riverside.

I decided on a 4/1 run/walk pace and was really pleased with the average pace, I'd definitely managed to increase the walking speed, 4.35 miles in 49min 21 sec.

We arranged to go to parkrun the following morning to do some more 3/2 pace and I have to say it's a lot easier running with someone else. Saying that, this session was a good run. It felt good to be able to just get out there with no goal or target in mind.

And yes... I have entered the ballot for the next London Marathon and if I don't get in, I'm thinking Manchester would make a good alternative!

So, have I persuaded you to get off the sofa this weekend yet? Even if it's just starting off with a walk it's a start.

LESSON: Remember that running should be about enjoying yourself, every so often just go for a run because you can, not because you have to.

What's that mean in English?

For all those of you like my mum who haven't got a clue, or for those of you like me who keep forgetting and have to look it up!

1 Mile	1.67 Kilometres
3.1 Miles	5k
6.2 Miles	10k
13.1 Miles	Half Marathon 21 Kilometres
26.2 Miles	Marathon 42.16 Kilometres

Contact Helen Stothard

You can follow my running blog here:

http://www.runfatgirlrun.co.uk

or follow me on Twitter at: @helenstothard

or you can drop me an email at helen@hlsbs.co.uk

I'd love to hear how you're getting on with your training.

So go on then...

... Run Fat Girl Run

...because if I can do it, anyone can do it!

6367768R00111

Printed in Great Britain
by Amazon.co.uk, Ltd.,
Marston Gate.